OURTOPIAS
cities and the role of design

Edited by Paola Poletto · Philip Beesley · Catherine Molnar

Canadian Design Research Network · Design Exchange · Riverside Architectural Press

Library and Archives Canada Cataloguing in Publication

Ourtopias / edited by Paola Poletto, Philip Beesley and Catherine Molnar

Published in partnership with the Canadian Design Research Network and the Design Exchange.
Includes bibliographical references.
ISBN 978-0-9809856-0-3

1. City planning.
I. Poletto, Paola, 1969-
II. Beesley, Philip, 1956-
III. Molnar, Catherine, 1978-
IV. Design Exchange (Firm)
V. Canadian Design Research Network

NA9040.O97 2008   307.1'216   C2008-902586-5

Design and Production: Hayley Isaacs and Philip Beesley
Cover image adapted from Toronto Rivers over time, Ravine City by Chris Hardwicke
Printing by Regal Printing Limited
This book is set in Akzidenz Grotesk and Swiss 721 Th BT

Copyright © 2008 Riverside Architectural Press
All rights reserved by the individual paper authors who are solely responsible for their content. No part of this work covered by the copyright herein may be reproduced or used in any form or by any means—graphic electronic, or mechanical, including photocopying, recording, taping or information storage and retrieval systems without prior permission of the copyright owner.

CDRN/RCRD
Canadian Design Research Network
Réseau canadien de recherche en design

ARCHITECTURE
WATERLOO ARCHITECTURE CAMBRIDGE

Preface

The Design Exchange, in partnership with the Canadian Design Research Network (CDRN) and Riverside Architectural Press is proud to present Ourtopias.

In 2007, the DX presented the conference 'Ourtopias', the purpose of which was to examine both the historical and contemporary cultures and contours of urban experience and the status and promise of the post-millennial, post-industrial urban fabric. This publication, Ourtopias, is a collection of original essays that present ideas about city making—past, present, and future.

Much has been written about cities—utopian or not—their doing and undoing. From Plato's Republic in 400 BC to the time that Sir Thomas More published Utopia, in 1516, and beyond—dreams about making an ideal society have spawned thoughts and considerations of perfected cities—with perfected legal and social systems—nestled in idyllic built structures.

However, at the DX, we propose 'OURtopias'—a play on words—which infers that the human experience cannot be removed from the city experience. In this context, is a Utopian city possible? No. Colloquially speaking, perspective is the litmus test. Perspective is individual, changes over time—evolves. And too often, in my opinion, it evolves into tunnel vision—preventing citizens, politicians, developers, designers and architects from creating a true Ourtopia—a city for the people, by the people—that strives toward reflecting the human experience: emotional, flexible, adaptable—reflecting the memories of its citizens and promising hope for the future. To create an Ourtopia, we must all get involved and act without ego—for the betterment of the future.

At the DX, we would like to dedicate this book to Moshe Safdie, creator of Habitat in Montreal's Expo '67, who has inspired us all with his publication, The City after the Automobile: An Architect's Vision, written with Wendy Kohn.

Samantha Sannella, BFA ID, M Arch
President and CEO, Design Exchange

CONTENTS

TORONTO

POSSIBILITIES

ACTION

PAOLA POLETTO PHILIP BEESLEY	03	Introduction
BRUCE KUWABARA	07	Ourtopia: Ideal Cities and the Role of Design in Remaking Urban Space
MASON WHITE	21	Condomania! Condominium Culture and Cities of Convenience
GLENN MCARTHUR	29	John M. Lyle and the Civic Improvement Committee: A Head, a Heart, and a Pulse to Toronto
IAN CHODIKOFF	41	Fringe Benefits: Cosmopolitan Dynamics of a Multicultural City
AKIN SEVINC	53	Beware! Traffic Ahead! Destination: Utopia
MARIA DEL C. VERA SHAI YESHAYAHU	59	From Urban Cell to Global Hive
ADAM KOLODZIEJ	67	Genius Loci: The Need for Urban Scenography
THOMAS SEEBOHM JOHN DANAHY	75	Towards Constructive Dialogue: Real-Time Visualization and Geographic Information Systems
JAMES KIRKPATRICK	87	Landscape Manufacturing
CHRIS HARDWICKE	95	Ravine City and Farm City
DOUGLAS MACLEOD LARISSA MULLER DAVID COVO RICHARD LEVY	109	Towards a Design Nation
ROBERT F. WOODBURY	121	Afterword
	123	Publication Credits
	125	Biographies

Introduction
Paola Poletto and Philip Beesley

The essays in this book were developed from presentations at the Ourtopias conference hosted by Toronto's Design Exchange in June 2007. City designers, activists, and legislators offered a widely varying focus that included poetic imagination, diverse public cultures, and practical methods for working with complex city forms. The essays gathered here probe how design affects the city today and how design can transform cities in the future. A quickened pace of urban development in Toronto provides the setting for the book, including rapidly increasing ambitions and scales in recent urban developments.

Toronto's original topography could be seen as vague, unmemorable. Its foundations are arguably thin—indeed the name Toronto is itself transposed from an Iroquois term, meaning 'trees standing in the water', named for Lake Simcoe about two hours away from Toronto's City Hall.[1] However, far from dwelling on provincial and marginal qualities, the authors in this gathering focus on potent and evocative images. These voices offer compelling visions that act as 'leitmotifs' for the renewed city: fine-grained tangled accretions in Kensington Market; the grand ambition of John Lyle's huge axial streets in his 1911 Federal Avenue plan; epic qualities of massive ironworks spanning Toronto's deep ravines captured by Michael Ondaatje's popular literature.[2]

A fundamental optimism runs through this book. The tone is evident in essays on engineered environments and integrated natural surroundings, and it also prevails in methodical reviews on participatory design process and municipal legislation. In a central piece, Bruce Kuwabara draws an argument for Toronto's 'renaissance', demonstrated in strong public investments in cultural institutions and growing resolve for sustainable development. Kuwabara broadens this picture by discussing recent initiatives of Vaughan, Winnipeg, and Ottawa in integrating green spaces and dense urban development. This kind of buoyant resolve might have been expected in 'City Beautiful' urban design proposals from early

[1] John Steckley in 'Scholar sole speaker of Huron Language' by John Goddard, **The Toronto Star** (December 24, 2007) (www.thestar.com/News/Ontario/article/288382)

[2] Michael Ondaatje, In the Skin of a Lion (Vintage Canada, 1996)

last century, but it can also be found here embedded within nuanced critiques such as Mason White's wry commentary on the architecture of condominiums, and Ian Chodikoff's compelling review of sprawling, ethnically diverse suburban commercial strips. White poignantly investigates the market and life-style-driven images of global condominium culture, suggesting that ideas of 'interior urbanity, extreme convenience, [and] homogeneous social programming' are at the core of this dominant building type. Chodikoff explores unconventional uses of buildings, strip malls, and streets in the suburban shopping streets of Scarborough, revealing a remarkable vitality thriving with micro-business commerce, worship, education, and cultural expression. Glenn McArthur's essay recounts examples of the City Beautiful movement within Toronto, giving a detailed review of John Lyle's major civic interventions at the beginning of the twentieth century. His paper details the design and development of Lyle's landmark Bloor Street Viaduct, describing how that epic form was influenced by international examples of grand avenues and by local ravine networks lying below the surface of the city.

Section two, 'Possibilities' begins with Akin Sevinc's survey of two centuries of visionary plans for cities. While the subject of utopian city planning is inevitably fraught, the authors here offer poignant sympathy for a shared future. Shai Yeshayahu and Maria del C. Vera's 'Global Hive' envisions the earth as a living organism. Adam Kolodziej takes us on a visual journey through lost cities and places, in search of 'genius loci'. John Danahy and Thomas Seebohm provide a review of visualization technologies that can enable wide participation in urban design, supporting direct collaboration between designers, community stakeholders, and policymakers. James Kirkpatrick speaks of the transformative power of green space in urban development, and compares current Toronto initiatives to the 'High Line' neighborhood in New York, which is giving rise to a new celebrity-injection lifestyle. Kirkpatrick argues that Toronto's new parks can outlast ephemeral city images, inviting the city to 'shift its identity from the vertical peak of its famous tower to the horizontal expanse of its park land'. Chris Hardwicke's 'Ravine City and Farm City' combines compelling rhetoric and wildly scaled ambitions. Hardwicke's proposals would expand Toronto's ravine network into an extensive labyrinthine wilderness, and integrate vast scaffold structures holding engineered farm terraces within a city of the future.

The final section of the publication, 'Action', examines how government legislation can support design. Drawing on the combined expertise of the Canadian Design Research Network, David Covo, Richard Levy, Douglas MacLeod, and Larissa Muller review policy initiatives from around the globe and discuss Canada's current approach to design policy, demonstrating the value that design can offer in global markets.

The conversations that created Ourtopias were born from remarkably vital ongoing dialogues within popular press and the Spacing, murmur, and readingtoronto communities working together with public organizations such as the Design Exchange and major design schools within the city. The refreshing optimism of these voices comes from an engaged, effective design community, deeply invested in the future of their city. They demonstrate potent possibilities for a thriving Toronto.

TORONTO

BRUCE KUWABARA	Ourtopia: Ideal Cities and the Role of Design in Remaking Urban Space
MASON WHITE	Condomania! Condominium Culture and Cities of Convenience
GLENN MCARTHUR	John M. Lyle and the Civic Improvement Committee: A Head, a Heart, and a Pulse to Toronto
IAN CHODIKOFF	Fringe Benefits: Cosmopolitan Dynamics of a Multicultural City

Ourtopia: Ideal Cities and the Role of Design in Remaking Urban Space

Bruce Kuwabara

What is 'Ourtopia'? Ourtopia is situated between an unattainable utopia and a dystopian future. Ourtopia is attainable through the transformation of the ideal into the real with a plurality of thought and action. It implies a vision of the city as open and in constant transformation for the better.

We are living in a moment of great change. Leaders and the broader public are facing the realities of global warming, poverty, AIDS, and world conflict. The Internet has propagated mass awareness that we have a limited amount of time to make critical course corrections. At the same time it has also provided a collaborative platform to harness ideas, and to innovate and generate solutions more efficiently and quickly than ever before. As designers, we have the potential to participate in driving change by producing exemplars of excellence that support human potential at all levels of creativity, work, and life.

This paper identifies specific conditions that position Toronto as a viable model for Ourtopia in the twenty-first century: acceptance of complexity and heterogeneity; an open-ended urban grid; the confidence to engage local and global talent; a vital public discourse on issues of urbanism and architecture; a thriving design community; the simultaneous revitalization and funding of cultural institutions and the city fabric; an appreciation for heritage fabric; and an annual cycle of cultural festivals. It concludes with a series of exemplars illustrating possible strategies for evolving the physical realm of Ourtopia.

COMPLEXITY AND HETEROGENEITY

John Ralston Saul in his book Reflections of a Siamese Twin argued that Canada is one of the most engaging contemporary models of democracy in

Facing Page
1 Canada's National Ballet School, Projet Grand Jeté: Stage 1–Jarvis Street Campus, Toronto

the world today. Canada, Saul stated, is strongest when it is open to complexity and heterogeneity.

To remain open-ended and non-conformist, to embrace people of different cultures and backgrounds and to allow them to exist as themselves is a fundamental condition of a civil society and therefore of Ourtopia.

OPEN-ENDED MATRIX

In 1788 Captain Gother Mann, an officer of the Royal Engineers in Upper Canada, applied the British surveyor military ordinance grid to organize the plan of Toronto.[2] Superimposed on a small area off the shore of Lake Ontario, between the land bounded by the Humber and Don Rivers, this gridiron pattern set the future direction for urban planning in Toronto, imposing an artificial rational order on a natural topography characterized by deep ravines and a rising terrain. Mann's gridiron eventually evolved into a super arterial grid—a flexible matrix responsive to growth, creativity, and reinvention pictured on the facing page.

Within the grid the main streets set the cadence of the quotidian rituals of life and work: along them we encounter culture and entertainment; we shop, dine, and hang out; we walk, cycle, drive, or take public transit. The issues that concern the public are played out here—debates about the integration of public transit; the quality of streets as places for neighbourhoods and communities to thrive; gentrification; and public safety. Along the major arterials, the street corners are critical to urbanity and set up conditions for the intensification of mid-block sites through various scales of architectural intervention.

The intimately-scaled Fresh restaurant by Giannone Associates engages its urban context with a floor-to-ceiling glazed entrance and generous windows to blur the boundary between the activity of the street with the restaurant inside. The Terrence Donnelly Centre for Cellular and Biomolecular Research designed by Behnisch Architects and architectsAlliance is a larger scale example of how buildings can be designed to engage street corners and activate urban contexts through the skilful integration of heritage contexts, the use of transparency and extended landscaping—in this case the south-west face of the University of Toronto's downtown campus along College Street.

In Ourtopia the grid or matrix promotes interconnectivity—of individuals, communities, institutions, economies, and events.

INSIDERS & OUTLIERS

Ourtopia welcomes both local and global scales as vital conditions for engaging citizens and leaders in debate and discourse on issues of city building, culture and the environment.[3]

The greatest advances in the quality of architecture in Toronto have occurred when the city has been open to external influences in all art forms. The current 'Cultural Renaissance' has created the most important architectural moment in Toronto since the 1960's—the last significant period when local and international forces converged to transform the city. Canadian architects such as Eb Zeidler (Ontario Place), Ron Thom (Massey College) and Raymond Moriyama (Ontario

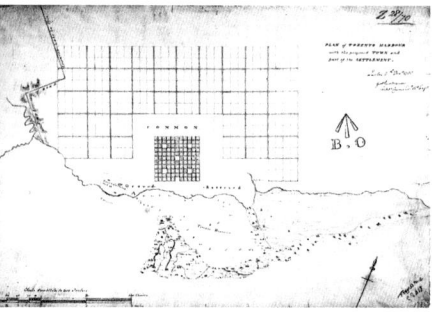

2 Gother Mann, Plan of Toronto Harbour, with the proposed town; and part of the settlement (1788)

3 Outliers is a term coined by William Thorsell to describe the international architects who have contributed to the transformation of the city.

Facing Page
4 Diagram of Super Grid by KPMB
■ Transforming Urban Precincts
■ Cultural Renaissance
■ Main Streets
■ Waterfront Developments
■ Waterfront Connections
☐ Arterial Grid

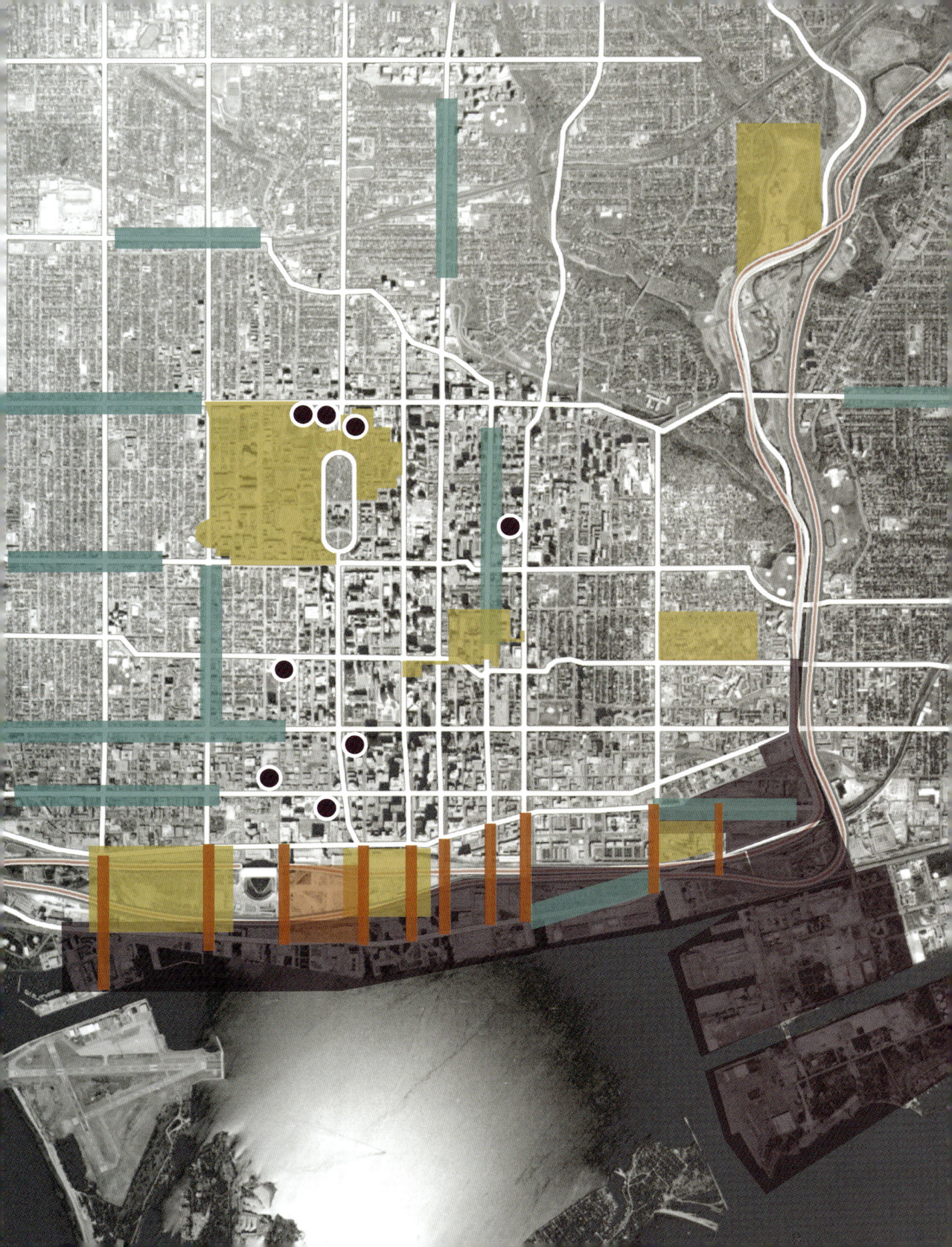

Science Centre) created projects concurrent with international architects such as Viljo Revell (New City Hall), Mies van der Rohe (TD Centre), and I.M. Pei (First Canadian Place). In the first decade of the twenty-first century Jack Diamond (Four Seasons Centre)[7], KPMB (Gardiner Museum, Young Centre, Royal Conservatory of Music) and others are creating projects concurrent with Will Alsop (Ontario College of Art & Design), Daniel Libeskind (Royal Ontario Museum)[5], and Frank Gehry (Art Gallery of Ontario).

The simultaneous development of these projects has recaptured the imagination of the city and stimulated a vocal public, passionate clients, visionary architects, and engaged patrons, critics, and citizens who cumulatively set high standards for excellence.

ACTIVE DESIGN COMMUNITY

In Ourtopia, designers lead change. In Toronto, the power of design to transform the city gained momentum with Will Alsop's Ontario College of Art and Design (OCAD). It was also OCAD that attracted the British publisher, Wiley, to produce Sean Stanwick and Jennifer Fiore's *Design City*—a book that documents the critical mass of designers and projects transforming the city at every scale: from cafés to hip hotels in renovated heritage buildings (The Drake by 3rd Uncle and The Gladstone by Zeidler Partnership) to retail shops (the Umbra Concept Store designed by Kohn Shnier) to healthcare facilities (Bloorview Kids Rehab by Montgomery Sisam/Stantec) to cultural and educational projects (from the AGO to MaRS).

SIMULTANEOUS CULTURAL PLATFORMS

Ourtopia produces opportunities to cultivate and display the power of imagination and creativity. Toronto's Cultural Renaissance was triggered by the Federal Provincial Infrastructure funding program initially referred to as the Cultural Superbuild. Its working premise was that refurbishment and expansion of our cultural institutions would increase cultural tourism. Toronto had lost bids for the Olympic Games, and was soon to be hit by the SARS outbreak of 2003. Our governments—municipal, provincial, and federal—finally acknowledged the importance of arts and culture to both the quality of life and the economic well-being of the city.

The Cultural Renaissance projects are proof that dreams can become reality. Each began with a unique vision. Each was led by committed directors, staff, and boards, and supported by the largest outpouring of private donorship for cultural development in the history of the city.

There are nine projects that I associate with Toronto's Cultural Renaissance. While they are all different, they all share the goal of providing a framework to cultivate and showcase human imagination and creativity.

- Roy Thomson Hall Enhancement[6]
- Canada's National Ballet School[1]
- Young Centre for the Performing Arts for Soulpepper Theatre and George Brown College[10]

5 Royal Ontario Museum – Michael Lee-Chin Crystal, Toronto

6 Roy Thomson Hall Enhancement Project, Toronto

- Four Seasons Centre for the Performing Arts[7]
- Royal Ontario Museum (the Michael Lee-Chin Crystal)[5]
- Gardiner Museum[14]
- Art Gallery of Ontario Transformation
- Royal Conservatory of Music, TELUS Centre for Performance and Learning[8]
- Bell Lightbox for the Toronto International Film Festival Group (TIFFG)[16]

Perhaps one of the important lessons of Toronto's Cultural Renaissance is that the institutions supported rather than competed against each other by uniting in their applications for government funding.

PUBLIC REALM

Ourtopia prioritizes a connected public realm. On the heels of the Cultural Renaissance is the simultaneous transformation of large-scale urban precincts and parks: University of Toronto and Ryerson University; Regent Park and the Distillery District; the Centre for Addiction and Mental Health (CAMH) and the Queen Street West district; the Railway Lands; the visionary Evergreen project for the Toronto Brick Works in the Don Valley; and the West Don Lands, and the East Bayfront, two new precincts being developed by the Toronto Waterfront Revitalization Corporation. The parks include Don River Park by Michael Van Valkenburgh (New York); Lake Ontario Park by James Corner of Field Operations (New York and Philadelphia); the Central Waterfront Park by West 8 (Rotterdam) and du Toit Allsopp Hillier (Toronto); HTO Park by Janet Rosenberg (Toronto) and Claude Cormier (Montreal); and the 8-acre urban park at Concord CityPlace on the Railway Lands West by Phillips Farvaag Smallenberg and Douglas Coupland (Vancouver).

To maximize the value of these investments in culture, city, and landscape, we still need a clear and compelling vision that reconnects Toronto's public realm to the waterfront. The Gardiner Expressway has to be addressed with a view to the long-term sustainability of the city and the investments in city building to date. If we can't tear the Gardiner down, let's build over it. Chicago's Millennium Park achieved a long-desired reconnection with the waterfront by building over active railroad tracks and a surface parking lot. Similarly Seattle's Olympic Sculpture Park by Weiss/Manfredi Architecture was built up and over the barrier of the existing transportation infrastructure to create a pedestrian 'art' landscape reconnecting the city's urban core to a revitalized waterfront. Both projects demonstrate the crucial role architecture can play in enhancing the everyday experience of the public realm, as well as invigorating civic pride and tourism.

MEMORY

Every building was once contemporary; every building implies a city: Ourtopia revalues its past. After watching Sarah Polley's *Away from Her*, Canadian journalist Robert Fulford wrote that victims of Alzheimer's are doomed to live in an eternal present, and questioned the value of life without memory. By extension, what then is the value of a city without the collective memory of a historic fabric?

Toronto, in the last century, acquired a notorious reputation for ruthlessly demolishing its landmark buildings and historic fabric. Is it a sign of Toronto's maturity then that of the nine Cultural Renaissance projects only two projects are stand-

7 Four Seasons Centre for the Performing Arts, Toronto

8 The Royal Conservatory of Music, TELUS Centre for Performance and Learning, Toronto

9 Canada's National Ballet School: Kuwabara Payne McKenna Blumberg Architects/ Goldsmith Borgal Company, Architects (joint venture architects); Radio City: architectsAlliance

Facing Page
10 Young Centre for the Performing Arts, Toronto

alone buildings—The Four Seasons Centre and the Bell Lightbox for the Toronto International Festival Group. The others—OCAD, Canada's National Ballet School, the Young Centre, the Gardiner, the ROM, the RCM, and the AGO—all involve interventions and integrations of existing building fabric.

FESTIVALS

Ourtopia encourages the human need to gather, celebrate, and imagine. In Toronto the array of cultural festivals is growing and enriching the seasons—from the Toronto International Film Festival and the all-night arts festival Nuit Blanche in September, to WinterCity in February, to Doors Open Toronto in May and Luminato, Toronto's first international festival of arts and creativity in June.

Luminato, a multidisciplinary arts festival which presents a spectrum of creativity, manifests the vision and energy of the Cultural Renaissance. First launched in June 2007, it attracted more than one million people to its programs and events. Many of the works that premiered went on to be staged abroad, such as the musical interpretation of Leonard Cohen's Book of Longing by Philip Glass. Cohen said that the project with Glass was less about collaboration and more like a collision: 'like that iceberg crashing into the [ROM] up the street.' Asked whether he liked the Glass piece, Cohen said that he thought it was beautiful and that it, the work, was better than both of them.

EXEMPLARS OF EXCELLENCE

Exemplars of architectural and design excellence in Ourtopia set directions for shaping the public realm and in ensuring a healthy civic future. The following projects in Toronto and beyond present a series of exemplars conceived to influence change and suggest sustainable conditions for building cities and communities.

ENSEMBLES OF OLD & NEW, PRIVATE AND PUBLIC: CANADA'S NATIONAL BALLET SCHOOL AND RADIO CITY

Canada's National Ballet School/Radio City development establishes a model for the harmonious co-existence of heritage and contemporary architecture and demonstrates broadly recognized urban planning principles that link the level of street life and diversity of activities to the level of safety in a neighbourhood.[9] The original goals were to catalyse the revitalization of Jarvis Street, Toronto's first upper class residential neighbourhood which had experienced long-term economic decline since World War II; to introduce much-needed home ownership options into a high-density rental market; and to stimulate community pride through its award-winning architecture.

The combination of residential landuse and institutional cultural amenities in one precinct illustrates a concept of urbanism that accepts and celebrates complexity, diversity, and seemingly contrary conditions to achieve urban transformation.

The massing strategy was co-authored to achieve maximum density on two urban blocks with shared courtyards and to integrate three heritage properties: the two slender point towers and the contemporary dance training centre are set back to respect the residential scale of Jarvis Street and to feature the heritage buildings on Jarvis Street.

11 Thomas Struth, **The Bernstein Family**, Mudersbach 1990, C-print, 108 x 134 cm, courtesy of the artist and Marian Goodman Gallery, New York

12 Richard Sennet, 'Recovery: The Photography of Thomas Struth,' **Thomas Struth: Strangers and Friends**, Thomas Struth, James Lingwood and Matthe Teitelbaum, eds. (MIT Press, 1994)

The contemporary German photographer, Thomas Struth, has been producing a series of family portraits such as the The Bernstein Family[11] since the mid-1980s. Richard Sennet, an art critic, in his essay 'Recovery: The Photography of Thomas Struth'[12] compares the human figures organized around a table to buildings in an urban setting organized around a shared public space. At an urban scale, Canada's National Ballet School/Radio City project offers a portrait of Toronto architecture and urbanism in the twenty-first century—with generations of architecture organized as an ensemble of old and new, solid and transparent, high-rise and low-rise, around shared open space.

MUTUAL ACCOMMODATION: THE GARDINER MUSEUM

In Ourtopia, new interventions revalue, relate and reinvent what exists. A friend and collector of Asian art, Bill Macdonald, spoke about the concept of mutual accommodation with reference to the Gardiner Museum renewal, a particularly Canadian concept which both respects the identity of the other and is a fundamental condition of civility. In architectural terms, mutual accommodation is about generating a dialogue between what is new and what exists.

The original two-storey Gardiner was designed by Keith Wagland in the early 1980's to zig-zag back from the street to protect views of an adjacent neo-classical limestone façade. One of the objectives of the renewal was to preserve the intimate scale of the original design and the planning principles which were conceived to protect views of two adjacent heritage buildings: the Beaux-Arts Lillian Massey building to the north (1908-12), and the eclectic Jacobean style Annesley Hall to the south (1901-03). The renewal strategy clarifies the existing plan, including the addition of a third floor. A new terraced landscape of low plantings and generous platforms creates an inviting and open public zone leading up to the entrance. The overall concept amplifies and re-imagines views and experiences of its surrounding urban history.

CIVIC LANDSCAPES: VAUGHAN CIVIC CENTRE

13 Vaughan Civic Centre, Vaughan

The Vaughan Civic Centre (2010) will be located in the community of Maple within the City of Vaughan. As a young city, it presents a case study in the consequences of rapid urban sprawl in absence of a unifying urban development plan. The objective of the Civic Centre is to set a direction for the environmentally responsible and civic-minded development of Vaughan in the twenty-first century.

The design concept is based on the idea of cultivating a civic landscape. The 30,193 m² program is distributed within a campus of low-rise structures organized to configure an accessible public terrain. The buildings and landscape are laid out in a series of east-west bands in reference to the linear pattern of land cultivation which formerly characterized the region, as well as the larger framework of the concession grid.

The project is targeting a LEED Gold rating, and integrates a high-performance building envelope, passive solar shading strategies, and maximum exposure to natural light and ventilation. A glazed clock tower acts as a solar chimney, drawing in fresh air at the building perimeter to reduce operating costs and reliance on mechanical systems.

14 Gardiner Museum, Toronto

PERFORMANCE AND AESTHETICS: MANITOBA HYDRO DOWNTOWN OFFICE PROJECT

Winnipeg is the coldest city in the world with a population over 500,000. It is also the sunniest location in Canada and boasts the hottest and most humid summers. Temperatures vary seventy degrees over a year, plummeting below -35°C in the winter, and soaring above 35°C in the summer.

The new 65,030 m² headquarters for Manitoba Hydro is located in downtown Winnipeg. As the fourth largest electrical utility in Canada, the design of the new building required exemplary energy efficiency and carbon emission reduction that would be second to none. A primary goal was to achieve 60 percent reduction below national standards for energy consumption, an unprecedented target for its scale and climate.

The Integrated Design Process (IDP)—a process that promotes a collaborative exchange of ideas and expertise at all stages—was essential in realizing the daunting project goals which intersect all areas of aesthetics, sustainable design, and energy performance required for a LEED Gold rating. The design concept was generated by the climactic conditions of Winnipeg: two towers converge at the north and splay open to the south to capture the maximum sunlight and strong southerly winds unique to Winnipeg's climate. The space between the towers is enclosed by stacked atria which act as both solar heat collectors and 'lungs' to fill the building with fresh air, 24/7/365.

The resolution of the array of objectives in a harmonious, integrated concept is an example of how corporations can lead positive change in environmental responsibility and improve the quality of daily life with healthy, supportive work environments, and engaging public spaces that ultimately contribute to building the city.

15 Manitoba Hydro Downtown Office Project, Winnipeg

SUSTAINABLE DEVELOPMENT: ROCKCLIFFE

The former CFB Rockcliffe is a 138 hectare site located in proximity to downtown Ottawa and the last large undeveloped property within the Greenbelt. Canada Lands Corporation commissioned an interdisciplinary design team (KPMB Architects and Greenberg Consultants, with Philips Farvaag Smallenberg and Barry Padolsky Architects) to develop a community concept which would integrate the regeneration of large-scale natural systems.

Site concepts for the new greenway system were developed following an in-depth analysis of the existing terrain, wildlife corridors, greenbelt restoration possibilities, and the potential to address storm water management. A priority was to achieve connectivity to surrounding communities, the Rockcliffe Parkway, the Aviation Museum, NRC, Montfort Hospital, and the existing Greenbelt trail system. The plan establishes eight small mixed-use neighbourhood precincts, all within walking distance of the town centre which comprises a market, public square, and main street.

The overall concept adopts an open-ended operative system as opposed to a resolved composition, to provide a series of strategies for the sustainable development of residential communities.

BODY OF WORK OVER TIME

Change is the result of many large and small interventions, renovations, additions, intensifications, transformations, and re-workings by teams and individuals over time.

For the last twenty years, KPMB has designed projects that have contributed to Toronto's urban fabric. The earlier work—such as Woodsworth College at the University of Toronto, King James Place on King Street East, and the Design Exchange—was modest in scale and urban presence, and often involved interventions to existing buildings, or interiors. In the past five years, the studio has had many opportunities to make a more visible impact, primarily through the numerous commissions for the Cultural Renaissance. This body of work reflects a particular urbanism with primacy on high standards of quality and excellence, building for the long term, and shaping the public realm.

TORONTO: AN EVOLVING OURTOPIA?

Open-ended, complex, evolving, Ourtopia prioritizes a sustainable, healthy, and civil future, and the basic human need to gather, imagine, and celebrate.

We all need to make critical course corrections of change to ensure human potential is supported at all levels of creativity, work and life—in the realms of business, culture, design, urban planning, sustainability, research, and education—both locally and globally.

To realize the potential of Toronto as an exemplar of Ourtopia we need to aspire to the permanence of cities that continue to have appeal—Rome, Paris, London, New York—cities built around harmonious urban form and space. To achieve this, we need to sustain the momentum of cultural and urban development. We need to continue to optimize our existing urban fabric, and the potential of the open-ended arterial grid. We need flexible platforms to allow our institutions to adapt to changing programs and needs. We need to inspire and encourage excellence from the development and design community. We need politicians who lead by example and get things done with prerequisite funding programs. We need leaders who are as passionate about culture and the environment as they are committed to the social and economic well-being of our cities.

16 Bell Lightbox–Toronto International Film Festival Group, Toronto

CONDOMANIUM!
Condominium Culture and Cities of Convenience
Mason White

> The high-rise was a huge machine designed to serve, not the collective body of tenants, but the individual resident in isolation.
>
> JG Ballard, High-Rise

In his 1975 novel High-Rise, JG Ballard chronicled the social breakdown of an affluent community living in a forty-storey high residential tower replete with supermarket, swimming pool, bank, and school. As the tower reaches 'critical mass', or full occupancy, the social stratification becomes destabilized and a battle erupts between lower and higher floor occupants. Amenity floors, stairs, and elevators—or, all that is shared—became grounds for territorial claims and tit-for-tat pranks. Ballard's part-social critique, part-architectural warning did little to stall proliferation of an already cemented building type. Nor did other popular 1970s criticisms of the skyscraper—Modernism's troubled offspring—such as the 1974 disaster film Towering Inferno, released following the opening of the Sears Tower in Chicago and the World Trade Center in New York.

In fact, the high-rise is a remarkably robust building type. With each blow, the skyscraper seems to return with ever greater momentum and strength. The massive construction boom following the events of September 11, 2001 is the most recent proof of this resilience. Initially declared outmoded after 9/11, the high-rise resurfaced as a vital seed in our rapidly urbanizing age. The high-rise resurgence has amplified the inevitability that more than half the world's population will live in cities. According to the United Nations Population Fund (UNFPA), 2008 will mark that paradigm shift.[1] And it is the high-rise that will serve as a crucial ingredient

---

1 'State of World Population 2007: Unleashing the Potential for Urban Growth,' **United Nations Population Fund**, (2007)

Facing Page
2 The February 2006 issue of **Toronto Life** featured a story about the 'Condo Generation'. Reprinted with permission by **Toronto Life** (St. Joseph Media, 2008).

LUST: SEX SHOPS, FROM STAID TO SLEAZY | **FOOD:** CHOCOLATE IS THE NEW WINE | **POLITICS:** BELINDA STRONACH'S UNIVERSE

TORONTO LIFE

THE CONDO GENERATION
COOL OWNERS // HOT BUILDINGS // GREAT DESIGNS

LIVING LARGE IN 700 SQUARE FEET

PLUS: WHY THE CONDO MARKET IS CRASH PROOF

$4.95 FEBRUARY 2006
www.torontolife.com

to accommodate this urban intensification. However, with its preference for autonomy, an abruptness to ground, and a tendency toward the iconic, the high-rise is in dire need of reconsideration.

Since its inception, the skyscraper has come to represent a city's ambition, economy, or population explosion. It peaked in the 1950s and 1960s through the technological innovations of the office tower. Curtain-walls, mechanical systems, and elevators assisted the office tower's rise into its rightful place in downtown cores.[3] The role and acceptance of the residential tower, however, has been far more complex. If the first two phases of the skyscraper depended upon technology and economy for its basis, the third phase seems to be aligned with less tangible interests such as media and lifestyle. This phase is finding its stride in the guise of the contemporary condominium.

Although stopping short of the dystopic conclusion of Ballard's science fiction, our age has realized a version of High-Rise all across North America—through the rise of the condominium as the domestic inhabitation choice 'du jour'. The condominium building establishes a complex cruise-ship-like social mix of mine and ours. It is property in the sky linked by a backbone of shared, communal spaces. The contemporary condominium presents a vertical enclave of convenience. It is a cocktail of hotel and apartment cooperative. It is social homogeneity that aspires to luxury and amenity.

CONDO ORIGINS

> Not since the late nineteenth century—when developers had to convince a wary public that apartment living was safe and appropriate for well-to-do families—has vertical living been marketed so aggressively and so conceptually.
> Penelope Green[4]

The vertical apartment building emerged out of a social necessity, equipping cities to house a burgeoning population during post-war American urbanization. However, the birth of the condominium was primarily an economic and legal one emerging out of a mix of common and civil law legal systems. Salt Lake City, Utah remains an unlikely host for the first condominium, but it was there that the 1960 Condominium Act effort of Keith B. Romney introduced it to a wider North American audience.[5] The 1960s witnessed initial condo development success in South Florida—because of an abundance of relocated retirees and its proximity to Puerto Rico, a trailblazer of condominium law—before spreading to urban centres across North America.

The 1970s and 1980s saw a rush to convert apartment buildings to condominiums or co-ops across North America, especially in New York City. These condos primarily established their character through finishes and, later, some experimented with amenities such as gyms. The condo market bottomed out in the early 1990s. And it wasn't until the late 1990s that a massive market interest in the condo returned with greater diversification and competitive designer-developer star power.

---

[3] For more on the office tower type, see Inaki Abalos and Juan Herreros, **Tower and Office: From Modernist Theory to Contemporary Practice** (Cambridge, MA: MIT Press, 2005)

[4] Penelope Green, 'The New Sky Shapers,' **Departures Magazine** (September 2006), 53

[5] Keith B Romney authored several editions of **Condominium Development Guide: Procedures, Analysis, Forms** (published by Warren, Gorham, and Lamont) between 1974 and 1990

Facing Page
[6] Proposed cover, Rem Koolhaas' **Content** (2003)

On par with New York, Vancouver has played a significant role in the evolution of the condominium type across North America. Two events particularly ignited Vancouver's high-rise boom: the 1989 purchase of the former World EXPO grounds, and the release of the 1991 Downtown Plan. These two have combined to make Vancouver's downtown peninsula North America's densest residential district.

Anticipating a large population increase following the impending hand-over of Hong Kong, the condo market accelerated downtown development. In 1989, Li Ka-shing, a Chinese billionaire, purchased an 82.5 hectare site formerly of the 1986 World EXPO. The area is called Concord Pacific Place and, at a cost of over $4 billion, represents North America's largest master-planned community. When it is completed in 2010, it will house approximately 20,000 people along Vancouver's waterfront. A slew of condominiums currently dominate the Yaletown and Coal Harbour districts of the downtown peninsula.

Vancouver developed the social-bonus zoning system, which offers increased density to developers in exchange for public benefits often in the form of social programs. This deal has led to a saturated downtown condominium district. Trevor Boddy, a critic of the 1991 Downtown Plan's outcome, has calculated that 'ninety percent of the nine million square feet of new towers approved in downtown during this decade have been condos.'[7] He likens this makeup to a 'dormitory suburb' suggesting that street life is not what you would expect given the density.[8]

Vancouver's condo massing is highly influenced by two references: the small-plate high-rise of Hong Kong towers, and a base podium of New York townhouses. As the Vancouver type migrated across Canada and the US, their small-plates widened, the tower shortened, and the podium extended. Toronto, as with many cities in North America, has elected to customize the type to suit its economy and urban fabric. However, the slender Hong Kong model became the fatter, squatter Toronto cousin.

It is more than mass and form that inform the type. Toronto, taking cues from New York and Miami, continues to be innovative in terms of programming. Several recent condo projects seek to combine cultural amenities within the complex. In some cases, such as Festival Tower and the Arts and Heritage Awareness Centre (AHA, currently known as the Hummingbird Centre), the podium is almost exclusively a cultural facility. The case of Festival Tower is also significant in its merger of private funding and government support boasting over $50 million from provincial and Canadian government funding. The proposed AHA Centre is designed to sit below a forty-nine-storey condo complex. It is hard to imagine condo towers directly atop new cultural institutions, but the idea of residential density adjacent to cultural destinies has been a trusted urban recipe.

In Toronto, four of every ten homes sold in 2004 were condominiums. It is estimated that about 3 million people live in condos across Canada. Condos have climbed from nearly one-fifth to nearly one-third of all new construction in Canada. From 2001 to 2005, condo starts posted an annual average increase of 16 percent.

[7] Trevor Boddy, 'Downtown's Last Resort,' Canadian Architect (August 2006), 20

[8] Ibid

BUYING A BRAND

Human specimens [are] neatly labeled by their consumption preferences.
Leanne Delap[8]

8 Leanne Delap, 'The New Starter Home,' Toronto Life (February 2006), 24

The condo proliferation in North American cities has spawned an advertising assault on home-seekers and investors. Marketing efforts promote condominiums as an amalgam of lifestyle and tourism. Probably no other building type or program is as entangled in marketing and advertising as the condominium. Entire magazines, with names like Condo Guide, Condo Life, and High-Rise, are devoted to sifting through the ins and outs of various condominium developments. The Toronto Star has even established a full section weekly that is exclusively for news related to condominiums. It is the only building type that typically has another temporary building, the sales centre, built in anticipation of its coming.

Current averages of development costs show a division of about five percent toward design and a whopping fifteen percent toward marketing. The total cost of a condo is more influenced by its marketing methods than its design. Developers flirt with branding strategies that showcase designer names and personas as if condominiums were product design, something you could buy off-the-self. Alluring 'be-with-the-in-crowd' lifestyle-based slogans are the vehicle that wills condo architecture into being. Each attempts to profile prospective buyers through the naming of the condo, the images of the promotional material, and carefully selected words and references on websites. Critical to this is the role that designers play in acting as marketable amenities themselves.

In Manhattan the recent explosion of condominiums is best represented by the marketing success of Richard Meier's all-glass 173/176 Perry Street completed in 2003. At sixteen stories, each raw floor sold for $8-12 million US, and then an interior designer was hired. Meier's name was the brand; the materials, glass, were the brand; and the address was the brand. For the Seventy5 Portland condominiums in downtown Toronto by Freed Developments Ltd., a different tactic was used. They enlisted Philippe Starck's development and design venture, Yoo, to design a signature vision for the project. Seventy5 Portland, like many designer condos, uses a particular design theme to seduce a particular buyer type. Some call it lifestyle profiling. Seventy5 offers two unit theme options, 'nature' or 'minimal,' encouraging a shopper's mentality of product identification whose dictum, 'I like it. It is me' perpetuates. The design is the brand; the lifestyle is the brand.

Many condo developments embrace the simulacrum of lifestyle. An excellent example is the Bohemian Embassy in Toronto's Queen West, a shabby chic outpost. The website states: 'Industrial-chic in architectural design and freethinking in spirit, Bohemian Embassy reflects the aesthetic tastes and artistic lifestyle of those attracted to Toronto's Queen Street West.'[9] The marketing is direct. It confesses to a 'reflection,' or simulation, of an otherwise naturally occurring phenomenon that is now immediately in jeopardy with such a blatant imposter next door.

9 Bohemian Embassy condominium website, www.bohemianembassy.ca (accessed June 12, 2007)

Alongside the unsurprising frenzy found in any competitive market is the long touted mantra of 'location, location, location.' Most condominium developments today find some angle, justified or fabricated, for pitching their location as an amenity. It is another form of branding, but this time at the scale of neighborhood. Sometimes it is about the street name, or a nearby park, or an existing or emerging commercial district. Sometimes, though, there is little location amenity, and this is where the developer stakes are high. This gamble has had a significant impact on the urbanization of the city's edges. Many exurban areas within the Greater Toronto Area (GTA), such as Brampton and Mississauga, have capitalized on this interest to populate their 'centres' with new residential towers in an attempt to generate a constellation of mini-metropolises.[11]

Nothing heralded this agenda greater than the Absolute Towers in Mississauga, part of the western GTA. Selected in an international competition, MAD office of Beijing posits a spiraling elliptical fifty-storey tower. The site for the project is an insignificant block in a horizontal, auto-centric exurban fabric. The project's success has spawned other condo developments immediately adjacent, creating an instant 'downtown' district comprised solely of condos. Typical of most exurban areas, nearby is Square One Mall, one of the largest shopping malls in Canada with 1.5 million m² of retail. The addition of the Absolute project to this area serves simultaneously as a brand, or icon, for a building and an urban centre yet to exist. Idealistic architecture and urbanism, the promise of the future, are even more 'brandable' before they exist.

CITIES OF CONVENIENCE

> Twenty-four hour room service, housekeeping service, laundry and drycleaning service, catered dining/events, valet parking, business centre and meeting rooms, screening room, rooftop infinity pool with bar/lounge, health and wellness centre, in room spa services, lobby bar restaurant, lower level bar/restaurant, personal trainers, pet services, private car service, grocery delivery.[12]

Central to the allure of condominium developments is their ability to internalize qualities of seeming urbanity. However, condominium urbanity is very different from the less predictable sidewalk-bound version of the city. Condominiums produce petri-dish urbanity. It is contained, controlled, and always room temperature. Once urbanism is invited to the condo interior, it is tamed, and becomes more sterilized and homogeneous. Its homogeneity is generated from the unwritten laws of economy and lifestyle producing a generic modern atmosphere.

More recently, the utilitarianism of amenity programs has been superseded with 'atmosphere amenities.' In a competitive market, developers are offering more than just functional amenities; they seek to offer something intangible. Not only are buyers subscribing to a physical place, but also, like a club, to an identity—an atmosphere. Condo development has reached such a competitive fever pitch that the one-upmanship of development has led to some of the most extreme examples of amenity-drenched living. The staples of gyms and pools have since expanded to include spas, juice bars, bowling alleys, and pet services.

---

[11] Larry Frolick, 'The Last Days of Suburbia,' *Walrus* (November 2005), 41

[12] From the 550 Wellington Condominium website, www.550wellington.com (accessed May 22, 2007)

Amenities offered suggest a complete service of convenience. One condo development states that it is 'like having your own private estate manager who deals with your apartment oversight so all you have to do is live there and enjoy yourself.'[13] This kind of service is primarily for the upper-tier condo buyer, but has trickled down to other developments as well. Condominiums are increasingly providing the very same services one would find in resorts or high-service hotels. The image of the condo presents a collective façade representing a club community. The 'atmosphere amenity' strand of the condominium market in North America is led by entrepreneurs who have previously established success in developing either hotels or nightclubs. No one has propelled this type of condominium development more than Ian Schrager and André Balazs. Schrager, a former partner in the 1977 founding of New York's infamous Studio 54, became a hotelier following the collapse of Studio 54. He developed Morgans Hotel in Manhattan in 1984, which has been considered the first boutique hotel. Balazs, much younger, began as an investor in nightclubs before becoming a boutique hotelier.

The boutique hotel peaked with two significant events—one considered a success and one a failure. The successful publication of several HIP Hotel books conceived by Herbert Ypma in 1999, documents 'highly individual places'—thus the H.I.P.—that are hotels. The criteria he has established for H.I.P. are atmosphere, attitude, mood, and tone. A boutique hotel is about selling an experience. Ypma marks the shift from the criteria of tangible luxuries to intangible luxuries in this part-guidebook, part-coffee table book series.

The collaboration of Rem Koolhaas and Herzog & de Meuron for a Schrager hotel at Astor Place in Manhattan around 1998-99 was, seemingly, a failed project. However, it solidified the role of design in the boutique hotels. The image of the design was more important than the actual design. These two design heavyweights, different in so many ways, were doomed to create a singular hotel. Koolhaas himself admitted that Schrager became 'increasingly uncomfortable' with their collaborative scheme.

Ian Schrager and Andre Balazs have taken the models of convenience and luxury to exclusive levels. Schrager is currently at work on 40 Bond in Manhattan, a luxurious condominium designed by Herzog & de Meuron. Balazs is currently at work on a condominium at 40 Mercer Street in Manhattan, with extreme luxury living designed by Jean Nouvel.

Condominium culture is immersive and presents domesticity as a totality that is hermetically sealed and at the service of comfort. Condos are like arks and just as replete with claims to having one (or two) of everything. Lifestyle is its measuring stick. Demographic is its angle. Convenience is its goal. The notion of interior urbanity, extreme convenience, homogeneous social programming, and mixed use will need to be central to re-thinking the role of condominiums in our urban age.

13 From the 40 Bond website, www.40bond.com (accessed May 24, 2007)

John M. Lyle and the Civic Improvement Committee: A Head, a Heart, and a Pulse to Toronto

Glenn McArthur

The beginning of the twentieth century was a period of intense rethinking of the urban landscape with elaborate proposals put forward in many cities across North America. The intention of these schemes was to address a wide range of urban issues in an attempt to create cleaner and healthier places for citizens to live and work; a goal which was to be achieved through a sense of order in both architecture and landscape. Like other North American cities, Toronto also generated many such utopian plans and urban renewal schemes with lofty goals of regenerating blighted inner-city areas, contributing lush green spaces to the urban fabric, and aesthetically improving the architectural landscape with buildings of heroic scale imbued with rich material and symbolic metaphor, which it was hoped, would contribute to its citizens' well being and civic pride. One of the major contributors of this period to this development in Toronto was the architect John M. Lyle (1872-1945). There are a number of aspects of Lyle's involvement with civic and urban matters that are worth examining. Not only did he design buildings for public spaces (he was one of the architects for Union Station), he also wrote numerous articles in architectural journals and newspaper editorials bemoaning the uncontrolled proliferation of visual street clutter produced by excessive store signage and telephone poles, and he proposed schemes to beautify the city's streetscape in order to attract the North American tourist. More than any other architect of his generation, Lyle worked hard at improving both the aesthetic and the functional aspects of the city. The two civic

Facing Page
1 John M. Lyle's reinforced concrete bridge proposal for the Bloor Viaduct (c.1911)

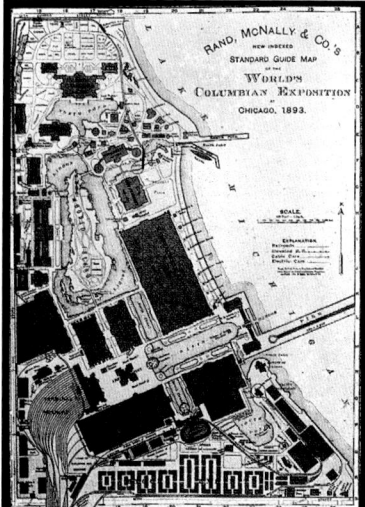

2   Fredrich Law Olmstead grounds and landscaping plan for the World's Columbian Exposition (1893)

3   'Notes–Concluded', Journal (6:4, April), xxviii

4   John M. Lyle, 'For Civic Improvement,' The Globe (2 February 1905), sec. 1, 2

5   John M. Lyle, 'Life History Notes, for Mr. S. Mathers,' unpublished manuscript (1945), 7. In the possession of Norah Harris, Victoria, British Columbia.

and urban design projects discussed here illustrate some of the contributions that Lyle made toward beautifying the city of Toronto.

John M. Lyle was born in Ireland, raised in Hamilton, Ontario and educated at Yale University and the École des Beaux-Arts, Paris. After completing his studies, Lyle worked in New York for nine years with some of the most prestigious firms in America. In 1905, Lyle set up shop in Toronto and through his architectural skills and a bit of good luck, established a practice that grew to be one of the largest in the city.

Through economic hardships and lifestyle changes, Lyle was able to produce a significant body of work that always expressed a highly personalized and original approach to architectural form and detail. He is perhaps best known for championing an authentic regional consciousness in building design, and attempting to pave the way for a uniquely Canadian architecture. In 1929, Lyle traveled to France in order to report on the modern movement that was sweeping through Europe. While disapproving of the more radical form of modernism, he embraced some of its features. This led to an idiosyncratic shift in his style and one that took him toward a regional Canadian design program for his buildings.

This phase of Lyle's work abruptly ended after the Wall Street stock market crash and the ensuing depression, which reduced the architectural program of every building to its bare essentials. But Lyle continued to transform and embraced much of the modern movement by simplifying elements, eliminating meaningless ornamentation, and being aware of the beauty that could be achieved through form, line, and colour.

Throughout his life, Lyle was actively engaged with a variety of cultural and professional organizations and served in an executive capacity as director, president, and member of the board of governors for numerous institutions. This included serving as the president of the Art Gallery of Toronto (the precursor of the Art Gallery of Ontario). In his professional capacity, he was an Honourary Member of the Beaux-Arts Society of New York, an Academician of the Royal Canadian Academy, a member of the Ontario Architectural Association (sitting on numerous committees), and he was made a Fellow of the Royal Institute of British Architects and the Royal Architectural Institute of Canada. Also, in recognition for his work in promoting civic and architectural improvement in Toronto, Lyle was elected as a member of the American Civic Association.[3]

Lyle's interest in urban planning and in beautifying Toronto became evident within weeks of his arrival in the city. After viewing an exhibition of proposed changes to the squares and bridge terminals of New York City by the architect Henry Hornbostel at the galleries of the Ontario Society of Artists, which was hosted by the Toronto Architectural Eighteen Club, Lyle wrote to the editor of a local newspaper commenting on the quality of the exhibited drawings. He then turned his attention to Toronto, writing, '...that Toronto is destined to become a city of world-wide importance is conceded on all sides, and now that there are so many projected public improvements the time seems indicated for great efforts to be made to draw up a scheme for the present and future beautifying of the city'.[4] Undoubtedly moved by Lyle's enthusiasm for urban planning, Sir John Willison, editor of the local Toronto News, requested him to write a series of articles on civic improvement for his newspaper.[5]

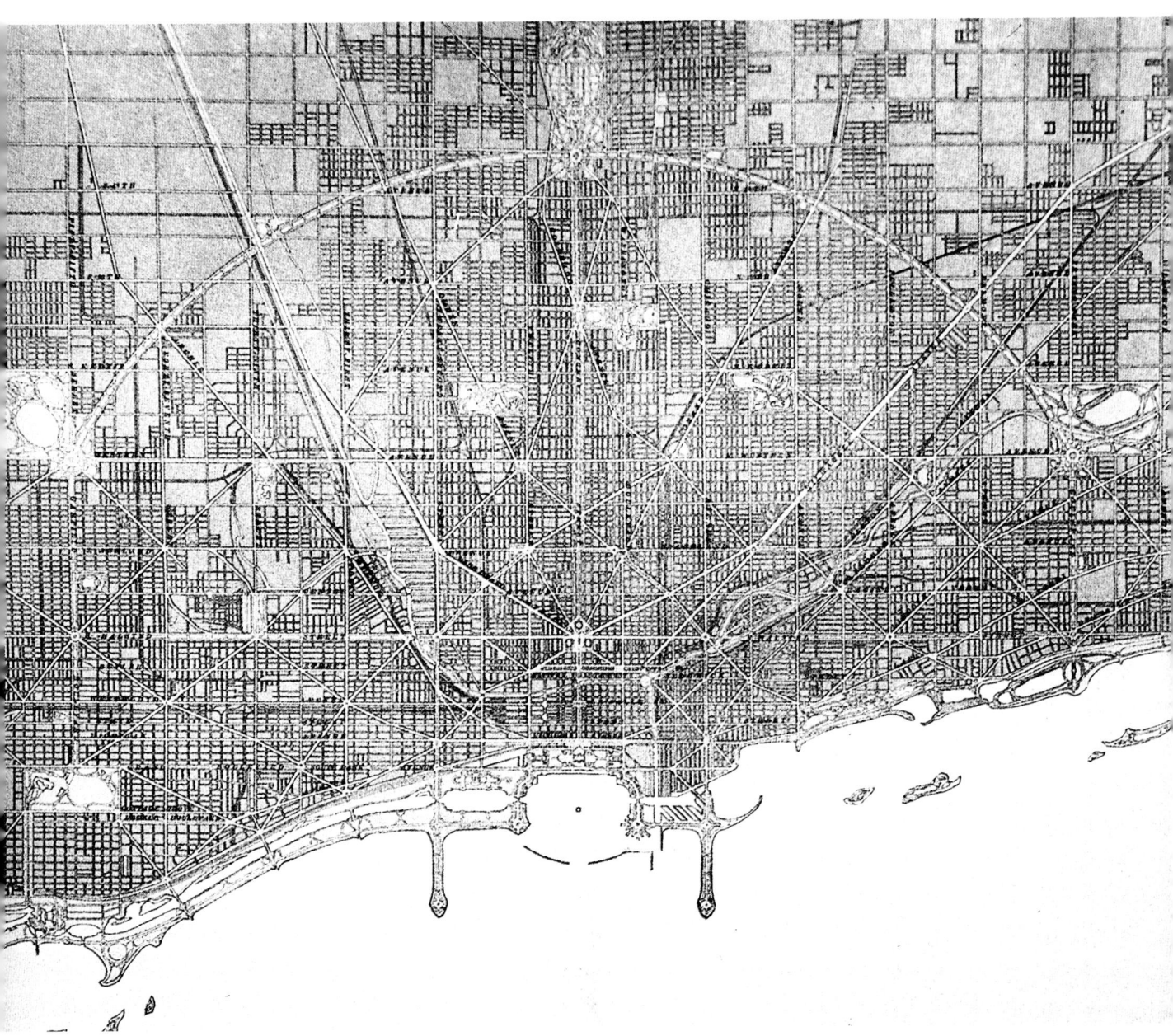

6 In 1909, Daniel Burnham's plan for Chicago included a diagonal roads system that radiated from an artistically embellished city centre, and a network of interconnecting roads and parks.

The issues and possibilities of urban planning that Lyle and other architects reacted to were sparked by the World's Columbian Exposition, in Chicago in 1893.

This exposition was primarily known for its impressive buildings. But what was to exert as much influence as the architecture was the site plan by landscape architect Fredrich Law Olmstead. The beautifully conceived grounds brought a greater public awareness to the possibilities of using urban planning and landscape design to help combat the unfettered and chaotic sprawl that was plaguing most North American centres. Olmstead was one of the first to enunciate the principles of the City Beautiful Movement, which evolved out of the need to make urban centres cleaner and healthier places to live and work through a sense of order in both architecture and landscape. As Canadian architectural historian Harold Kalman noted, the City Beautiful Movement had an 'enormous impact on American and Canadian urban planning for the next generation'.[7]

Due to the influence of the Chicago Exposition, many American cities began to beautify their own communities. In 1901, the city of Washington, D.C. engaged Daniel Burnham, Charles McKim, and Fredrick Olmstead, Jr., to study their park system, and in New York, Julius Harder proposed an urban scheme in 1905. Working independently, Burnham was also involved in preparing plans for San Francisco, Cleveland, and later Chicago, with designs that included diagonal roadways cutting through the usual urban grid pattern, as well as civic squares, and parkways.

In Toronto, where the population of the city had doubled between 1900 and 1912, there were also a number of concerned planning advocates attempting to beautify the city, and guide and control the nature of its development. Spearheaded by architects, businessmen, lawyers, and politicians, there were three groups working to achieve these goals: the Guild of Civic Art (later the Civic Guild), the Ontario Association of Architects, and the Toronto Architectural Eighteen Club. These organizations hosted lectures and wrote articles promoting the themes of urban planning, land use segregation, and a reworking of the city's grid pattern with the use of diagonal avenues, that were being put forward in various American cities.

At the 1906 Ontario Architectural Association convention, William A. Langton, who was a member of the Civic Guild and editor of the magazine Canadian Architect and Builder, tabled a report recommending the development of a radial road system similar to the ones proposed for Washington and Chicago. The plan was well received within the architectural community but Mayor Emerson Coatsworth was less enthusiastic, commenting that as far as politicians and ratepayers were concerned, the impending sewage system held a higher priority.[8] Bloodied, but not beaten by the lack of political support for their scheme, the Civic Guild continued to refine their plan. In 1907, they received a small grant from the city to hire British architect Sir Aston Webb, who had worked on the Mall approach to Buckingham Palace in London to help them with their quest.[9] Despite the raised expectations about the infusion of such a high-profile architect into the project, little was accomplished, and the Civic Guild's revised report of 1908 contained minimal changes. A year later however, having received further information from those members of the planning committee who, in the past year visited Washington, Philadelphia, and Baltimore, the Guild finally produced

---

[7] Harold Kalman, A History of Canadian Architecture (Toronto: Oxford University Press), 651

[8] James Lemon, 'Plans for Early Toronto, Lost in Management,' Urban History Review 18 (June 1989), 14

[9] Canadian Architect and Builder 20 (March 1907), 47

10 Plan of the Suggested Development of the City of Toronto (Guild of the Civic Art, 1905)

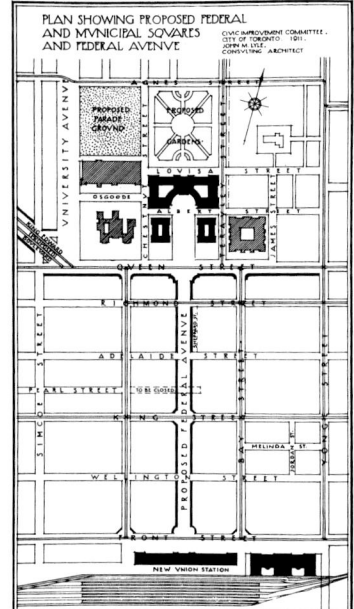

11 Plan Showing Proposed Federal and Municipal Squares and Federal Avenue, Civic Improvement Committee, John M. Lyle, consulting architect (1911)

12 John A. Ewan, Report on a Comprehensive Plan for Systematic Civic Improvements in Toronto (Toronto: Toronto Guild of Civic Art, 1909), unpagenated forward

13 Report of Civic Improvement Committee for the City of Toronto (Toronto: City of Toronto, 1911), 5

14 Lyle, 'Life History Notes,' 7

15 Construction (July 1911), 53

Facing Page
16 Union Station in the foreground and the Federal Custom and Exercise Building in the background

17 Don Valley looking north with Danforth and Broadview avenues on the right (c. 1913)

an impressive brochure outlining their hopes and aspirations for Toronto. Arguing that civic improvement and city planning were the remedies for the evils of congestion, they noted that 'thirty-nine American cities are now adopting, to a greater or lesser degree, a systematic plan for future development'. They bolstered their case by pointing out that the other cities' proposals were similar to the Guild's, in that they all called for 'wide continuous business thoroughfares, parks, parkways, playgrounds, aquatic sports, pure water, sanitary sewage disposal, rapid transit, clean streets, underground wires, curtailment of sign and noise nuisances, building laws for structural, sanitary and fire safety and tenement laws to restrict the congestion of population'.[12]

In response to the continuous lobbying of the Civic Guild, the mayor and city council created a new body in 1909 to 'prepare a comprehensive plan for the improvement of the City', and so the Civic Improvement Committee was born. It had many of the same members as the Civic Guild, but arranged itself into four sub-committees. These sub-committees included Lyle and fellow architect Edmund Burke.[13] Lyle was also appointed as the Committee's consulting architect and was, as he wrote later, 'given a room in the tower of the City Hall, in which to prepare our drawings'.[14] This appointment was a mixed blessing for Lyle, as it put him in a potentially compromising position. As a member of the committee, as well as its architect, there was the issue of a potential conflict of interest, since in some situations he would have to sit in judgment of his own work. To resolve the issue, Lyle resigned his committee membership and was rehired as the Civic Improvement Committee's architect for a salary of $1,000 per year, plus twenty-five dollars per week for his draftsman.

In 1911, the Civic Improvement Committee presented city council with over forty recommendations. These included some that were much the same as earlier proposals, as well as a design for the Bloor-Danforth Viaduct. Its most interesting recommendation, and the one which created the most excitement, was a majestic boulevard called Federal Avenue. The avenue was to be situated between Bay and York streets, beginning at Union Station—which would serve as a portal into the city—and terminating at an imposing Civic Centre to be located where Nathan Philips Square now stands. In the grand plan, Beaux-Arts classical buildings lined both sides of the boulevard, a Toronto equivalent to Chicago's White City. It also called for public gardens behind the proposed legislative buildings and a military parade ground next to the then existing Armouries on University Avenue. In Lyle's words, if carried out as planned, 'it will give a splendid setting for our public buildings; give open spaces and plaza for public demonstrations; eliminate slum conditions now existing in St. Johns Ward; relieve the downtown congestion; give a fine new business street to the city—in short, a head, a heart, and a pulse to Toronto'.[15]

The Federal Avenue scheme was the largest proposal by the Civic Improvement Committee, the majority of recommendations being more modest and practical, including street widening at a number of major intersections, some of which were implemented.

Few of the grand schemes that were proposed for North American cities by various Civic Improvement Guilds came to fruition. In Canada major schemes

proposed for Montreal, Ottawa, and Calgary met with similar fates. Apart from the prohibitive cost, most communities came to realize that city planning was more than a paper Beaux-Arts project; that it was a process, not of instant creation, but of slow gradual development. In Toronto, as elsewhere, the city did very little. Considering that the gains did not obviously offset the costs, that most elected officials were not motivated by the proposed changes, and that taxes for large public work projects had to be decided by public referenda, these results are not surprising.[18] However, the lack of tangible results did not discourage Lyle from future participation with political and architectural bodies, although they did not receive the full attention that they did during this period in his career.

Lyle's attempt to infuse the city with a head, a heart, and a pulse, as reflected in his proposed Federal Avenue plan, did have a modest legacy. Although his plan was not implemented as such, his ideas of having a grand avenue of classically ordered buildings forming a visually coherent streetscape, with Union Station as its focus, was partially realized. The federal government, who owned the site on Front Street between Yonge and Bay streets, had long been encouraged to participate with a large public building that would conform to Lyle's proposed scheme. They responded with the Federal Custom and Excise Building, originally selecting the site in 1911, but not designing and constructing it until 1929-35. The building's plans adhere to the gentle curve of Front Street, and in terms of aesthetics, reflect the grand Beaux-Arts design of Union Station. Dominating the streetscape, these impressive buildings represent a high water mark for Beaux-Arts and City Beautiful aesthetics in the country, and hint at what might have been, if Lyle's urban plans had been fully realized. Another portion of Lyle's scheme has serendipitously emerged through the on-going development of the subterranean network of walkways (PATH) and retail shops that connects Union Station with the civic buildings on Queen Street. Although not on the grand scale of the proposed Federal Avenue, its utilitarian nature makes for a highly functional pedestrian thoroughfare system that is utilized year round.

One large project that Toronto's politicians could not ignore was the proposal for a Bloor-Danforth Viaduct. There had been, for some time, a grassroots movement of local east-end business interests and commuters to connect Bloor Street and Danforth Avenue, which were separated by the Rosedale Ravine and the Don Valley. By 1910, the newspapers were heavily promoting a scheme that would connect these streets with a viaduct, while the city's engineering department was pushing for a steel bridge that would span from Sherbourne Street in the west, to Broadview Avenue in the east, in one continuous straight line. This scheme would have transversed over the Rosedale Ravine and the Don Valley, ignoring its natural beauty and cutting through the existing residential community.

The Civic Guild opposed the plan and prepared to put forth an alternative proposal consisting of John Lyle's plans. These plans called for a continuance of Bloor Street eastward, along a land-filled terrace section overlooking the Rosedale Ravine, and continue with two bridges. One bridge would start at the head of Parliament Street, span the ravine, and continue through to Castle Frank Crescent. The other bridge would cross the Don Valley and connect into Danforth Avenue. Lyle presented these plans to City Council at a meeting that was heavily

---

18 Lemon, 'Plans for Early Toronto,' 11

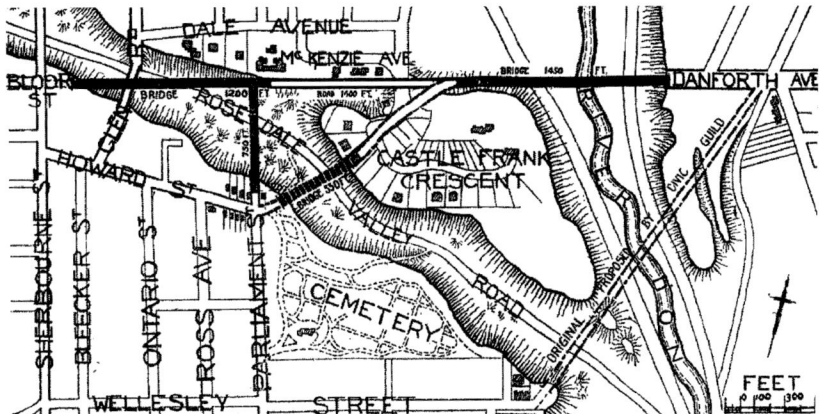

19 Proposed Bloor Viaduct design (c.1911)

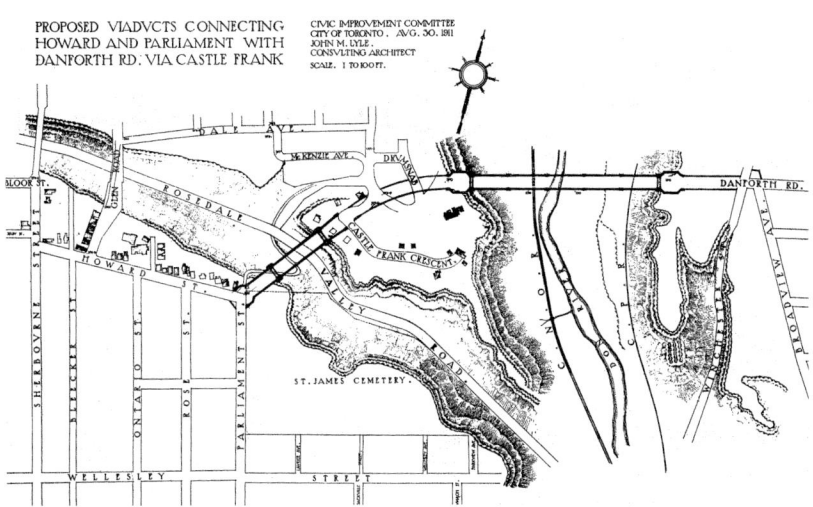

20 Proposed Bloor Viaduct route showing Bloor Street terminating at Sherbourne Street (1911)

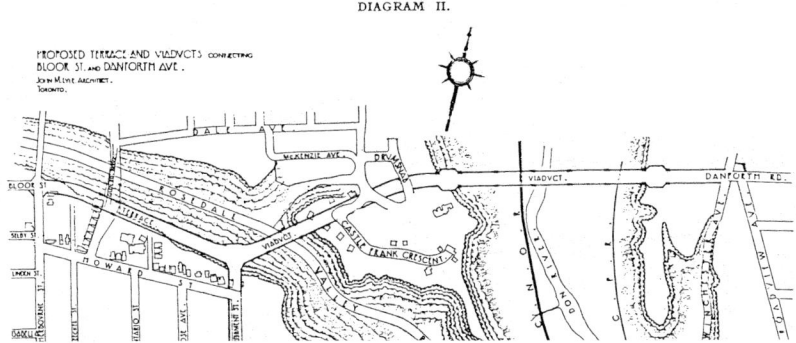

21 Bloor Street continuing over land filled area to Parliament Street (1913)

22   John M. Lyle's reinforced concrete bridge proposal for the Bloor Viaduct (c.1911)

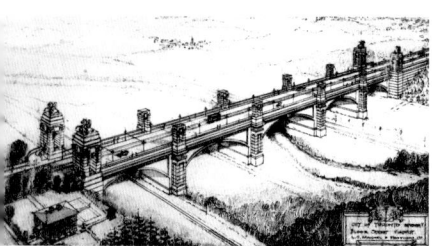

23   Proposal for the Bloor Viaduct by L.G. Mouchel & Partners Ltd., civil engineers, London, England (c.1911)

24   Lyle, 'Life History Notes,' 9

25   Ibid

26   Ibid

attended by the supporters of the straight bridge proposal. As Lyle noted, 'It was quite evident that the proponents of the straight viaduct down the centre of the ravine would ask for an early vote and an adoption of their plan'.[24] After listening to the arguments in favour of the straight viaduct however, the Mayor allowed Lyle to explain his scheme to council and show his drawings. Convinced by Lyle's arguments, the Mayor decreed that there should be further study of the whole problem, appointing a special committee to examine the different proposed schemes, and report to City Hall in a year. This Special Committee included local politicians as well as architects Edmund Burke and Lyle, as a result of which, Lyle spent, 'the whole of one autumn and winter tramping through the different areas affected along the Rosedale Ravine'.[25]

The following year, at a special meeting, thirteen different plans were submitted and each proponent was given fifteen minutes to present their scheme. After it was his turn to present, Lyle, as he described it '…sat down and prepared to hear a lot of objections. To my astonishment Billy McLean [editor of the Toronto World newspaper] got up and said that Mr. Lyle had given nine reasons why he considered his scheme the best route to be adopted and that while he himself had always been in favour of the straight viaduct, he would withdraw this support and stand behind Mr. Lyle's scheme. I cannot remember what else happened at the luncheon, but from our point of view it was a great success'.[26]

Lyle however was not awarded the commission to design the Bloor-Viaduct Bridge, although he had determined the layout of the roads, terraces, and bridges for the viaduct, had prepared a design for the Parliament Street Bridge that was exhibited at the Toronto Architectural Eighteen Club in 1909 and, along with two other engineers, had submitted design proposals. The reasons were probably political ones, as the design responsibilities were given to

27 Proposal for the Bloor Viaduct by Hedrick and Cochrane, consulting engineers, Kansas City, USA (c.1911)

28 Bloor Viaduct bridge shortly after completion in 1918

Edmund Burke, who worked with the City Engineer's office as an architectural consultant for bridges. Construction began in 1915, progressed very rapidly, and was completed by 1918.

Lyle was extremely pleased with his work and the completed project, with one exception. His original plans had called for terraced and landscaped areas along the north of Bloor Street from Sherbourne to Parliament, overlooking the ravine. These areas, suitable for bandstands and public promenades, similar to Dufferin Terrace in Quebec City, were not, to his regret, included.[29]

29 Lyle, 'Life History Notes,' 9

Fringe Benefits: Cosmopolitan Dynamics of a Multicultural City

Ian Chodikoff

We are all familiar with—at least superficially and anecdotally—the variety of ethnic and cultural groups found across the inner and outer suburban rings of the Greater Toronto Area (GTA). However, beyond our infatuation with postwar suburbs and near-academic curiosities associated with sprawling ethnocentric malls, architects must improve their visual literacy and develop a greater understanding of the multitude of adaptations to our suburban environments being initiated by a range of ethnic and cultural groups living in the GTA. Beyond the phenomenon of signs being printed in multiple languages and the renaming of streets to satisfy local business improvement associations (BIAs), the global influences placed upon our built environment are contributing to a welcomed introduction of higher densities and a desire to diversify land-use in suburban communities while expanding local economies and secondary real-estate markets such as wholesale distribution centres and forty-year-old strip malls. These factors are contributing to the cosmopolitan dynamics within our multicultural city, furthering the potential of making the GTA a leading model for urban development and evolution in the twenty-first century. This new discourse must be acknowledged and understood by architects and urban designers as they learn to anticipate and respond to ongoing design challenges associated with our globally networked amalgamation of disparate populations known as Toronto. Moreover, this new methodological lens requires an ability to recognize visual cues from the everyday functions of our urban contexts as future trends relating to physical urban change that can already be experienced in various communities across the GTA.

Facing Page
1 Thorncliffe Park, a Greek Orthodox church juxtaposed with a high-rise apartment complex

2 Taken outside of one of many strip malls along the Bathurst Street corridor, this photo represents one of many examples whereby different ethnic restaurants, shops and services can coexist.

Responsive and anticipatory planning frameworks resulting from what many cultural and ethnic groups have already set in motion will facilitate a more stable civil society, enable our diverse communities to remain connected to the world and pursue, protect, and expand upon solid principles of inclusionary urban development. We demand a framework that does not segregate and discriminate members within a particular ethnic group nor subjugate one ethnic group in favour of another.

CULTURAL SHIFT

The geography incorporating the GTA as a 'Creative City' extends beyond the stereotypical spatial limits attributed to a multicultural realm comprising of downtown Toronto, leaving the suburbs to exist as a cultural wasteland. As Shawn Micallef argues in uTOpia 2, the suburbs can actually become a creative incubator for the arts. For Micallef, Toronto's 'downtown has done a fairly good job in self-mythologizing, while the suburbs are, as suburbs tend to be, quiet and unassuming,' while adding that:

> Much of that diversity isn't strolling along Queen West every day. It exists outside of the core, living in these clusters and turning our generic strip malls into the main streets of the United Nations. These neighbourhoods are closer to Trudeau's vision of multiculturalism... and they may inspire art that incorporates new mash-ups of these various cultures.[3]

3 Shawn Micallef, 'Arturbia?' *The State of the Arts: Living with Culture* (Toronto: Coach House, 2007), 316

Thus the suburban landscapes along Jane Street, the Bathurst Street corridor, Dixon Road, Don Mills, and in Brimley are feeding Toronto the creative elements that are actually making it the cultural city that we aspire to be, despite the fact that we are often unaware that much of our creative energy emerges from communities outside the downtown core.

4 In suburban residential communities like this one in Milton, the hundreds of ethnicities that coexist are not easily visible behind closed doors

The politics of contemporary Canadian society may have rendered the terms 'multiculturalism' and 'globalization' meaningless. In a recent article appearing in The Toronto Star, architecture columnist Christopher Hume interviewed Corrado Paina, the executive director of the Italian Chamber of Commerce. Paina argues that cities like Toronto need to move beyond these truisms, noting 'In the western world, there are no cities that aren't multicultural. Immigration has always taken place. Multiculturalism is a concept that isn't serving people any more.'[5] Emphasizing his point, Paina explains that multiculturalism has become something more akin to cultural festivals, ethnic food fairs, and traditional forms of music. We have to come to terms with the idea that Little Italy is no longer Italian. It is time that we moved our interpretation of contemporary Canadian society further and where our politicians consult citizens from different backgrounds in the name of good business practices, not in the name of multiculturalism.

5 Christopher Hume. 'Antiquated notions can take us only so far' The Toronto Star (April 19, 2007)

COSMOPOLITAN WORLD

The word 'cosmopolitan' is derived from the Greek word 'kosmopolitês', which means 'citizen of the world'. The essential, shared ideals of cosmopolitanism is that all human beings from all groups, regardless of their political affiliation, belong to a single community contributing to a civil society based on political or social norms (i.e., the concept of Canada). K. Anthony Appiah's definition[6] of cosmopolitanism is something very different than what the city of Toronto may be accustomed to discussing. Appiah's argument essentially tries to understand the impact of modernity on societies with long traditions being carried forward into contemporary cultures such as what is exhibited in urban amalgamations like the GTA. Appiah argues that it is best not to enforce diversity onto our populations, nor confine the various elements of our citizenry who are trying to escape their

6 Kwame Athony Appiah. Cosmopolitanism: Ethics in a world of strangers. (New York: Norton, 2006)

Facing Page
7 During the annual Taste of the Lawrence in Scarborough, various ethnic and cultural stakeholders celebrate their diversity along Lawrence Avenue for a few days during a street fair with hawker stands and amusement rides. One might imagine how these kinds of manifestations will evolve over time.

8 Zygmunt Bauman. Globalization: The Human Consequences (New York: Columbia University Press, 1998)

9 Thomas L. Friedman. The World Is Flat: a brief history of the twenty-first century (New York: Farrar, Straus and Giroux, 2005)

10 Anthony Giddens. Runaway World. (London: Routledge, 2000)

11 Arjun Appadurai serves as Senior Advisor for Global Initiatives at The New School in New York City, where he also holds a Distinguished Professorship as the John Dewey Professor in the Social Sciences. For more information on ethnoscapes, see 'Global Ethnoscapes: Notes and Queries for a Transnational Anthropology,' Interventions: Anthropologies of the Present. R.G. Fox, ed. (Santa Fe: School of American Research, 1991), 191-210

past, or, who simply wish to improve their lot in life. Cultures continuously change, and this is what our society depends on for growth and development. There is a virtue in preserving a wide range of human conditions, allowing for our citizens the best chance to thrive. Appiah contends that cultures are made of continuities and changes. The identity of cultures that survive in a society is dependent upon its ability to support change. Societies exhibiting no change will fail to remain authentic and thus become dead societies. Within our own Canadian postmodern diaspora of cultures, the importance of people becoming used to one another across national, ethnic, and religious borders should be encouraged. For example, there are Chinese restaurants in Toronto that are halal, and are thus acceptable to a Muslim adhering to certain dietary restrictions in accordance with his or her religion. In this instance, Chinese food is no less acceptable than any other cuisine, so long as it is halal. Therefore, a kung pao chicken rice is no less valid to a Muslim than shish kebab. To refute this, is a revocation of cultural evolution.

In our twenty-first century liberal society, not only are we more ethnically diverse than we once were, but we are increasingly interconnected and interdependent. The implication of these shifts is what political theorist Zygmunt Bauman[8] refers to as 'glocalization'. The GTA is a definitive glocalized economy able to attract increased flows of capital from around the world. This is manifested with ambitious investors from Dubai who want to build fifty-storey skyscrapers in Markham, or by Bangladeshi immigrants who are focused on developing their global-networked mercantilist skills. Increased labour migration, improved connectivity through efficient methods of communication and technology, and a greater ease and use of affordable long-distance travel are helping to perpetuate the inexorable shift of Toronto toward a fully functioning twenty-first century global city.

Toronto is also experiencing what Thomas Friedman describes as the 'flat earth',[9] a world where increased social, political, and economic contacts are more easily achievable and where technology has lowered the barrier to entry for many people. Adding to this phenomenon, Anthony Giddens refers to our increasingly connected world with terms that seem to suggest a fracturing of geography. Referring to a 'distanciation' or 'disembedding' of our society, Giddens views our contemporary social relations as no longer linked to a particular place, and where our social relations are less tied to local contexts of interaction.[10] The result is a phenomenon where the social structures found within the GTA are recombined into various ethnically based communities extending across national boundaries while clearly manifesting themselves into a sophisticated network of semi-autonomous local communities—both socially and physically.

Reconsidering the urban-suburban amalgamation of such networked communities across the GTA, the implications of reconceptualizing our understanding of multicultural communities is what Arjun Appadurai[11] refers to as 'ethnoscapes'. Ethnoscapes are simply social landscapes created by ethnic group affiliations, and are only fortified by effective and vibrant immigration patterns constantly reinforcing a global connectedness with their ethnic centre—be it Teheran, Colombo, Hanoi, or Hong Kong. Such communities exist across the GTA, and many of them have access to high-levels of economic strength and intellectual capital.

12 On Canal Street in New York, a variety of informal and formal commerce developed by ethnic minorities have an eventual effect on the built environment, such as occupying abandoned lots with temporary markets

Politicians and planners alike are learning to acknowledge the potential of transnational migration patterns. With Toronto's foreign-born population hovering at 50 percent, a considerable amount of the GTA's population manage to live in two worlds at once—moving back and forth between Canada and the rest of world—managed either through the maintenance of a physical link through periodic travel, or by building social capital through family and community relationships. The GTA is a portal for thousands of trans-nationals—and so the concept of trans-nationalism is no longer new. If anything, the GTA is a definition of the term itself. Despite the food fairs such as those along Toronto's waterfront, the municipalities across the GTA have yet to methodically incorporate diversity and multiculturalism into their urban planning and design methodologies. Perhaps an explicit urban planning response is not the answer. Perhaps a more strategic approach is required of designers to resist formalizing the simultaneous processes of assimilation and entrenchment of individual identities.

What should emerge, as a priority for designers, is the necessity to construct mappings that consider our various ethnoscapes—or cosmopolitan territories—across the GTA. The implications of this cultural and physical mapping exercise will anticipate effective design solutions within the rubric of contemporary planning responsibilities that include the health, welfare, and public good of our communities. The value of this exercise will allow planners to facilitate a richness of the spatial possibilities resulting from a wealth of creativity emerging across the GTA.

Linking our evolving cosmopolitan identities and ethnoscapes with urban design opportunities will optimistically improve the co-mingling of private and public enterprise, entrepreneurial zeal, and social equilibrium. These are some of the challenges the design community will encounter when actively engaging in an increasingly sophisticated spatial understanding of Canadian multicultural activities across the GTA. As a result, architects must quickly develop a toolkit to better understand the processes affecting the development of contemporary architecture associated with multicultural shifts that will enrich the definition of what an urban fabric means to the traditional, if not benign, definition of a multicultural Canada.

CONTEMPORARY DESIGN RESPONSES

To understand the evolution of multicultural communities across the GTA over the past twenty years, a distinction should be made between inner and outer suburban rings of development. The inner suburban rings are those south of Highway 401 and Highway 7 and include areas like Don Mills, Flemingdon Park, and Scarborough. These communities take their initial shape and infrastructure from the postwar period and are thus working toward their third and fourth generation of occupation. Outer suburban rings were essentially greenfield developments twenty years ago and are thus working on their second or third generation of occupation. They include communities like Richmond Hill, Mississauga, Brampton, Markham, and Vaughan. Many incredible relationships exist between social networks, social capital, social exclusion, economic disparity, and entrepreneurial activities found amongst the various built environments across the GTA. What is required of urban planners and urban designers is the ability to observe and anticipate these shifts and evolutions in our suburban physical environments.

13 Each yellow-painted gas line represents one restaurant or food kiosk inside the vast and sprawling Pacific Mall in Markham, a successful mall that caters to Markham's largely Asian community

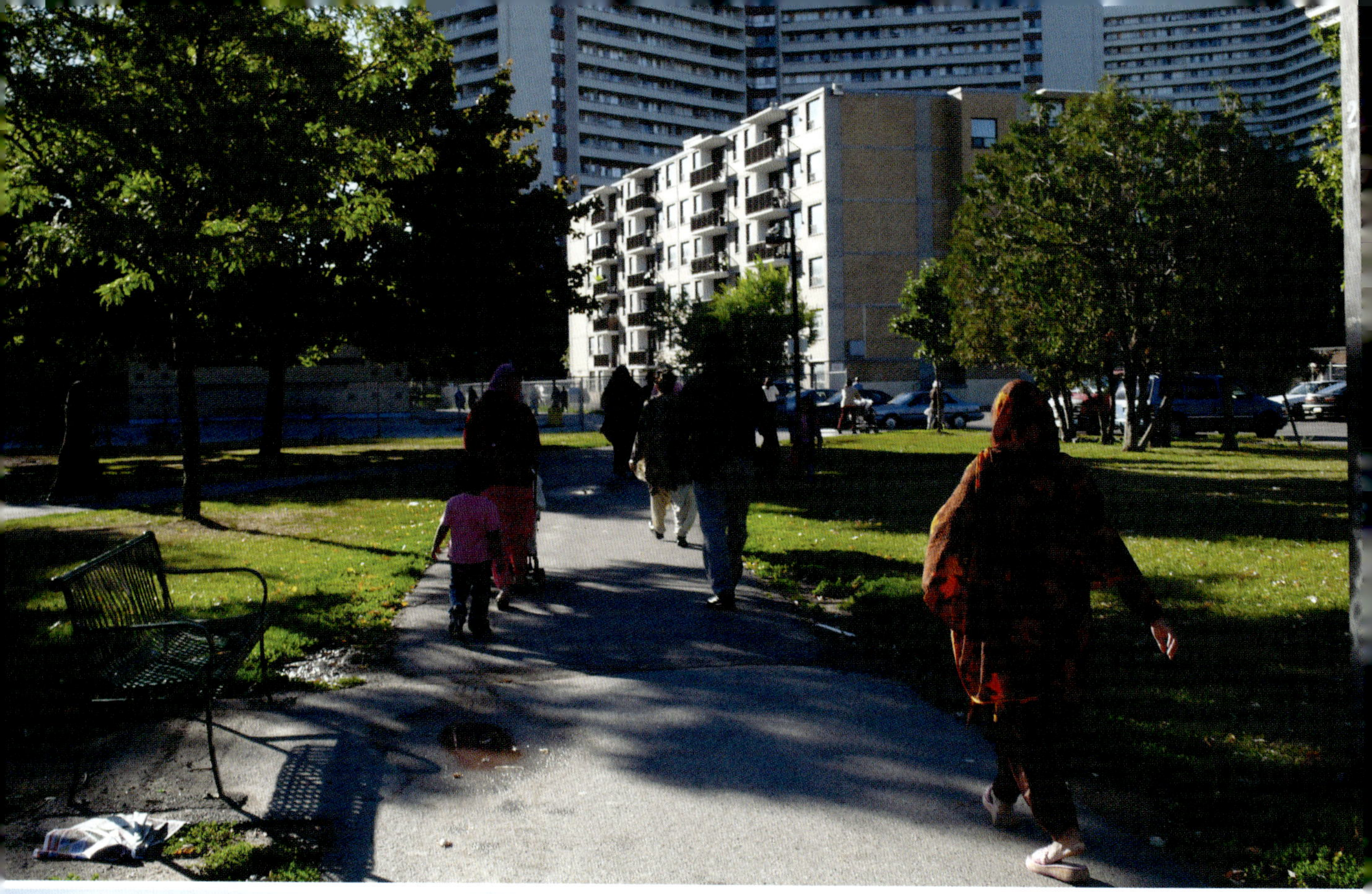

Belyea Bros.
MASJID DARUS SALAAM
مسجد دار السلام
Islamic Society Of Toronto
4-Thorncliffe Pk. Dr. Tel: 416-467-0786

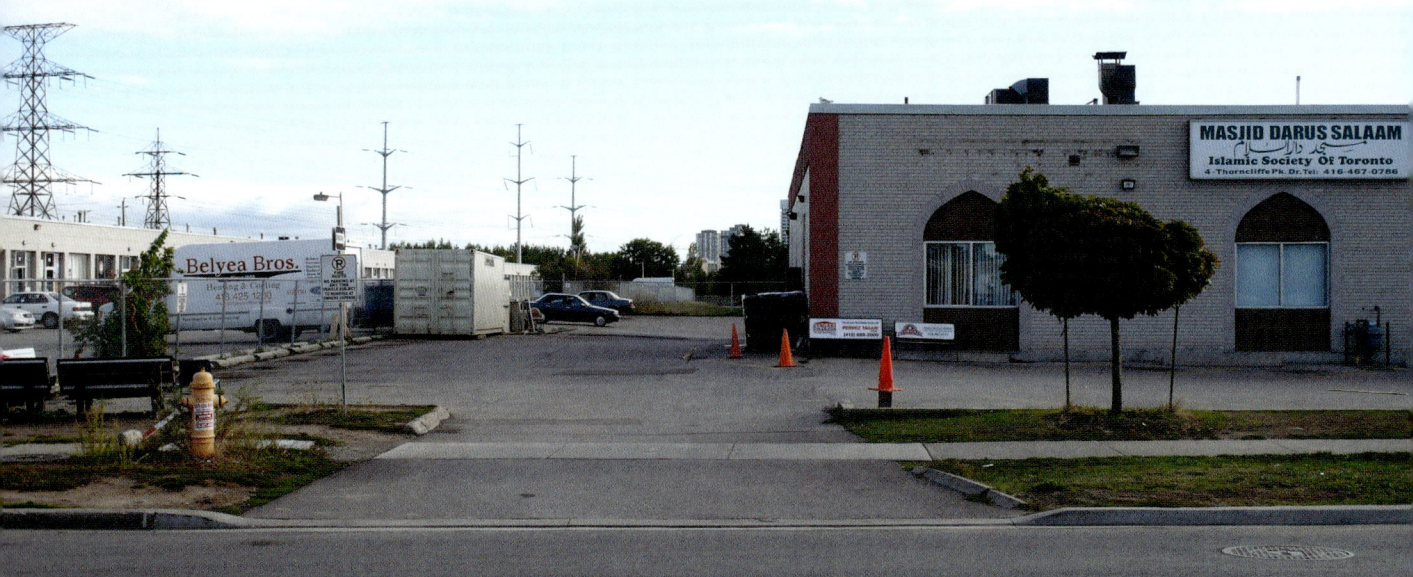

The assumptions and methodologies relating to the analysis of suburban occupations, appropriations, expansions, and mutations of these various swathes of suburban architecture and urbanism include everything from rehabilitating postwar suburban buildings and infrastructure to enriching the quality of the built environment through new approaches in landscape urbanism. Examples of residential buildings of various densities, commercial buildings of various forms, and cultural landscapes in a variety of scales are also due for intense discussion, documentation and speculation.

Architects must learn to adapt to evolutions throughout the various ethnoscapes of Toronto. Some of the conventional approaches associated with urban planning should be abandoned as designers become increasingly accustomed to:

14 Community gardens located in Thorncliffe Park

i   Responding to rapid and fluid mutations of commercial, retail, and residential configurations that will ultimately form the physical foundations for cultural activities of various multicultural groups (i.e., the Chinese malls of Markham);

ii Learning how to respect, reinterpret, and disseminate the changing needs of specific communities (i.e., evolving with a particular constituent's rising socio-economic status); and

iii Learning to shift design needs of cultural groups from the private to the public sphere (i.e., recognizing that as median incomes and political influence of a constituency grows, so will the desire to increase philanthropic measures and exert visible design manifestations within the public sphere).

There are already a considerable number of projects and urban design schemes being generated across the GTA that merit discussions pertaining to an evolving—and hopefully enriching quality of life found within various GTA suburban communities. The initiatives and intentions of architects, who are working within the GTA to recognize and respond to needs of various groups, signals an already extant level of sophistication in a formative approach to contemporary urban design processes.

THE FUTURE

Our suburban communities are not very old, but the social capital contained within them dates back many centuries. The relatively rapid development of our suburban communities and diverse municipalities across the GTA contains a significant inventory of architecturally and historically important buildings worthy of conservation and preservation. In addition to their rich cultural and architectural heritage, there is a burgeoning cultural capital growing amidst these communities as a result of ethnic diversity. Moreover, the process of informal urbanism being developed within these communities is exhibited not only by a wide variety of entrepreneurial efforts, but also through several contemporary responses by architecture firms who are responding to their own definition of what a suburban community entails.

The question of what constitutes a Global City should be rephrased as 'what constitutes a global-city region?' The effects of a cosmopolitan city-region will have enormous implications on the future face of the GTA. If architects and planners can respond appropriately, the GTA will emerge as a unique urban agglomeration that defines its spatial awareness through facilitating its connections to the world.

Facing Page

15 Located in East York, Thorncliffe Park is home to the largest concentration of Muslims in Canada. Here, in addition to community gardens or a Greek Orthodox church, one finds masjids located in industrial buildings and a popular community park set in amidst a series of apartment blocks.

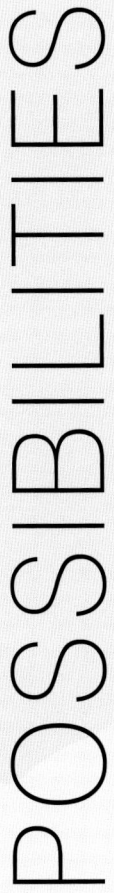

POSSIBILITIES

AKIN SEVINC	Beware! Traffic Ahead! Destination: Utopia
MARIA DEL C. VERA SHAI YESHAYAHU	From Urban Cell to Global Hive
ADAM KOLODZIEJ	Genius Loci: The Need for Urban Scenography
THOMAS SEEBOHM JOHN DANAHY	Towards Constructive Dialogue: Real-Time Visualization and Geographic Information Systems
JAMES KIRKPATRICK	Landscape Manufacturing
CHRIS HARDWICKE	Ravine City and Farm City

Beware! Traffic Ahead! Destination: Utopia
Akin Sevinc

Architectural utopias lay sketch paper over our urban places and offer brand new designs for living. Their objective is to create ideal spaces by transforming problems. However, utopias also warn and caution us against dangers. Just as road signs warn us of sharp curves and signal us to slow down or change direction and destination, the examination of proposed utopias highlights potential dangerous scenarios. Designers dream of navigating a city without subjecting it to environmental damage, and creating utopias with future-state transportation systems solidifies our dreams and gives us hope in a pessimistic world.

Beginning with Thomas More, imaginary projects have highlighted transportation and its role in shaping utopias. In More's Utopia, conceived in 1516, transportation criteria emerge as a determining factor in the design of cities and in identifying the status of these cities in their countries. 'The streets are very convenient for all carriage, and are well sheltered from the winds … There are fifty-four cities on the island, all large and well built, the manners, customs, and laws of which are the same, and they are all contrived as near in the same manner as the ground on which they stand will allow. The nearest lie at least twenty-four miles' distance from one another, and the most remote are not so far distant but that a man can go on foot in one day from it to that which lies next to it.' Whether identifying an ideal end-state or proposing criticism of King Henry VIII's state infrastructure (as some scholars suggest), More's thoughts give us insight into the plight (and sheer human determination) of creating livable cities.

One of the first people to emphasize the need for alternative solutions to transportation problems was Saint-Simon, a prominent utopist of the nineteenth century. In his study entitled Systéme Industriel, he states that transportation and carriage infrastructures are the basic determinants in the shaping of cities. Believing that transportation channels and industrialization were accelerating urban growth, he suggested new development plans for France, which focused mainly on easing transportation problems. After Saint-Simon, many others adopted his thoughts and took important steps towards building roads, water channels, harbours, and widespread railroads. Among the many projects inspired by Saint-Simon's ideas are the Panama Canal built between two oceans, the Paris Metro, and the tunnel beneath the English Channel.

Until the twentieth century, none of the utopias—except those of Saint-Simon—gave transportation problems a central role. Transportation did not emerge as a priority design criteria in any of these idealized models. However, when a functional and orderly living space is designed, it automatically puts forward a set of suggestions about transportation: plans including a grid system, straight streets cutting through cities, parallel streets, geometric forms, and so on. The common point in all these urban plans is the role they give to transportation networks. Street systems form a blueprint into which the basic functions of the city can be placed.

Known for his studies on urban utopias, Robert Fishman stated that the technological inventions of the early twentieth century such as the express train, automobile, telephone, radio, and skyscrapers inspired the architectural utopias of the time. Fishman underlines the emphasis placed on transportation in the imaginary projects of prominent utopists such as Ebenezer Howard, Le Corbusier, and Frank Lloyd Wright: Howard's emphasis on the need for railroads in balanced and well-planned cities in his project entitled Garden City (1902), Corbusier's belief reflected in his Contemporary City (1922) that 'streets in the air' created by skyscrapers acting as vertical streets would one day eliminate the problems caused by 'soulless streets', and Wright's idea mentioned in Broadacre City (1958) that well-designed roads and cycle paths are fundamental to the healthy development of cities. Fishman wrote that all three utopists mentioned transportation as a problem likely to be experienced in cities in the near future and they designed their projects as a solution.

Another important project in the early twentieth century was Antonio Sant' Elia and Mario Chiattone's An Aspect of the New City in 1914. Designed as a lively city, it takes its inspiration from vehicles: 'dynamo and power to the piston'. In this project, transportation is given more importance than other components, and it is this 'machine-like' quality that takes the city over and makes it lively.

In the 1960s, the heyday of architectural utopias, many projects proposed creative and unrivalled transport solutions. Having raised different questions about the transportation problems of cities, each one of these projects take us from the drowning city traffic and offer us a long and enjoyable trip to imaginary projects.

1   This project consisting of a transportation ring around Vetheuil, a city on the banks of the River Seine in France, suggests new accommodation units to be built in the mountains surrounding the city in addition to the city itself (Designed by: Equipe MIASTO, Michel Lefebvre, Jan Karczewski and Witold Zandfos, 1970)

2   A new scientific and technological interpretation of the traditional city, this project made from tensile structure aims mainly to solve traffic problems in the high-density cities of the future (Designed by: Frei Otto, 1957-1963)

3   Designed for downtown Moscow, this project leaves the city center intact and surrounds it with a two-storey circular service structure called the 'A Ring' and re-connects work and accommodation areas (Designed by: V. Kalinine & Y. Ivanov, P. Kovaliov, V. Maguidov and V. Tarassévitch, 1966)

4   Based on the idea of building giant structures in the slums of Harlem, this project aims to see the inhabitants of slums move into the giant buildings, and then transform slums into parks and other public areas (Designed by: Richard Buckminster Fuller and Shoji Sadao, 1965)

5   As a result of the attempt to make old cities co-exist with their new additions, this research project places the old city in its center and surrounds it with high-density 'shield' cities (Designed by: Chanéac, 1963–1968)

When a new transportation system is designed, does a new and ideal city appear? This question lay at the heart of the project entitled Manifestation Plastique.[1] The transportation system, surrounding the city and intended to operate partially with air pressure, offered different solutions: express roads, roads for slow driving, secondary roads, and arched roads connecting the secondary roads to living units through vertical connections. The city was intended to connect to the outside world via a rail system which intersected with a crossroads that brought together all roads. Highways and airports were located far from the city center.

Is it possible to have a city with massive areas for pedestrians and no entrance for cars? The project known as Future Cities[2] sought the answer to this question. Any river that runs through a city plays an important role in the shaping of the urban landscape. The river here would be used for transportation and at the same time provide the city with social gathering areas on its banks and bridges. The city plan featured an inner transportation system facilitated by cable-cars. Each cabin would accommodate four passengers, move on a line 4.20 meters above the ground, and work as silently as possible. Pedestrians, too, were transported by conveyor belts. In order to create an ideal city for pedestrians, cars would not be allowed into the giant tent.

When a city's major transportation problems are resolved, can it recover its past health? The project known as Redevelopment of the City Centre in Moscow[3] aimed to solve the transportation problems of Moscow with new architectural designs. The designers started the design process by identifying the following problems: first, the waste of time in people's commute between their work places in the city center and residential areas, and second, the frequent interruptions in the transportation system due to this high mobility. The project envisioned that the ground floor of one of its buildings, the 'A Ring', should be kept free for car parks and free flow of traffic. With its circular form, this two-storey building connects the city center to the 'bridge buildings' suggested in the project. In order to go to the city center, the inhabitants are expected to go to the 'A Ring' by train and then reach the center and walk around easily in the low traffic density.

Can a city's transportation network and car parks be hidden inside its buildings? The project called Slum-Clearance Scheme for Harlem, New York,[4] started with a different question from other projects. Attempting to radically change the city's social and architectural identity, this project was based on including roads in giant structures and using ramps to carry them to the top of buildings. The three-lane ramp-like roads inside the buildings are used for different purposes. One lane was reserved for climbing, the other for descending, and the last one for parking. The plan called for these huge buildings to be connected to each other with six-lane roads.

Can there be a way to leave the negativities caused by the transportation system outside the city? The project called Crater City[5] offered a transportation system consisting of different roads for different types of vehicles. The roads were to be placed outside a 'curtain' surrounding the old city, thus separating traffic and city life. The roads could then overlook buildings on one side, while the other side would overlook vast spaces and nature. Another suggestion of the project was a rail system: connecting the old city to other places via underground. Envisioning air travel as the only way of transportation within the cities of the future, the project left space for the conversion of roads into workshops and stores in the future. Special areas for helicopters and manned rockets were also featured in this project.

Can new transportation arrangements help bridge the gap between family and work life? Trigonic Spatial Cells[6] aimed to bring together all communication, production, and distribution functions within a well-planned transportation system. The design attempted to negotiate work and family life. Double-storey roads suspended with steel ropes from towers formed the carriage system of the building. Pedestrian walkways were given priority in the design: bridges built between main units allowed for pedestrians to walk around freely.

Can precautions be taken for future transportation problems caused by rapid urban development? Plan for Tokyo[7] was a design inspired by the developments after the Second World War. After WWII, Tokyo was thrown in chaos and planning was utilitarian—characterized by a strict urban grid and ultra-densification. Attempts to decentralize Tokyo were thwarted as the Japanese people clamored to be close to the city centre. In response, The Plan for Tokyo protruded from the city center over the sea to the Bay of Tokyo and would accommodate five million people. In order to make sure that the new part of the city and the center of Tokyo were well connected and retained their liveliness, a structure called Naval Cord was suggested to arrange and manage the traffic. Additionally, with an understanding that there could be future transportation problems in the city, several more solutions were offered: elevated multi-storey roads and railroads were connected to one another—and to airports under or over the sea.

How can we stop unhealthy urban development in the areas around ring roads? Instant City (Linear Pyramid City)[8] was planned over the highways surrounding existing cities. It was imagined as two equilateral triangles leaning against each other, both of which would be 200 meters long and 16.5 meters wide. The city would consist of high-density accommodation, work and—to a limited extent—rest/recreation buildings. The project thus aimed to restore urban accommodation relationships disrupted by fast transportation roads.

There is no completing this journey before stopping by the few projects that tackled the transportation problem a little differently than the perhaps more 'practical' utopian projects mentioned above. The popular claim about utopias being 'up in the air' becomes a reality observed in these projects rather than just an abstract cliché. The following four projects introduce designs which fly, hang 'up in the air', and have minimum contact with the earth. They position themselves far from transportation problems.

6 Designed for post-industrial societies, this city design is based on efficiency, allows for individual hobbies and stays in continuous contact with nature (Designed by: Yoichiro Hosaka, 1965)

7 'Plan for Tokyo' (Designed by: Kenzo Tange, Arata Isozaki, Koji Kamiya, Heiki Koh, Noriaki Kurokawa and Sadao Watanabe, 1960)

8 Designed by considering fast highways, this project is based on the idea of allowing vehicles to drive under buildings (Designed by: Stanley Tigerman, 1968)

9 Comprising mobile urban units connected by corridors which can be removed when necessary, this project is made of giant containers that can house an entire city (Designed by: Archigram (Ron Herron), 1964)

10 Inspired by a helicopter and fully equipped to fly, this project includes a cockpit, living room and bathroom (Designed by: Guy Rottier, 1965)

11 Aiming to transfer big scale industrialization to architecture, this project makes creative and diverse use of buses like caravans, and thus enables more diverse use of people's spare time (Designed by: Guy Rottier, 1966)

12 A no-gravity space city project modeled on the idea that cities will be built in the outer space in the future (Designed by: Paul Maymont and Renée Sarger, 1962)

What innovations may be achieved by making the city go for a stroll, stop at different points, and then make it stroll again? Walking Cities[9], for example, was designed around the novel idea that parts of the city can be moved with the help of wheels on its legs that lock into place. Why would helicopters not be used as homes? Flying Residence (Maison Volante)[10] was designed as a 4.90 m x 2.90 m helicopter-like vehicle which would bring together the ideas of transportation and accommodation.

May the future hold a life in which humans will always be on the road? Inspired by what caravans offer people, Bus City (Cité Autobus)[11] made both transportation and accommodation more enjoyable. 'Flexibility', which marks the projects of this period, comes together with 'mobility', thus creating a movable and re-shapeable project. By offering a travelling architecture, it aims to encourage people to adopt a new lifestyle: the life of a traveller. The possible 'traffic' problem of too many caravans gathering in the same place is avoided by creating a system whereby they will be loaded on top of each other.

What kind of problems may be awaiting us in a space city? Sketches for a Space City[12] envisioned one: as the city of the future may be built in a place with no gravity, a carriage system would become responsible for keeping the buildings in place. The attitude of the project towards transportation is surprising. There is detailed information about how space shuttles will reach the buildings and how they will park. The project emphasizes various serious transportation problems seen in the cities of the time, and helps us understand the disruptive relationship to its inhabitants.*

It is obvious that most of these architectural utopias were designed carefully so as to avoid any transportation problems. When we look collectively at the suggestions made about transportation especially in the utopist projects of the 1960s, we can reach the following conclusions:

- Transportation systems and living areas are designed as far away from each other as possible. Likewise, transportation networks, which are considered to be the prime reason for the failure of cities, are built as far away from living areas as possible.
- City centers are like little havens for pedestrians. Vehicles are not allowed into the city center so that pedestrians can move about freely.
- Railroad systems are a necessity. The projects seem to have come to a consensus about building rail systems under the ground.
- There is a continued search for alternative transportation means. Seas, rivers, or lakes are consistently proposed for transportation.
- It is a common belief in many utopian proposals that all transportation would be done by air in the future. Some of the projects thus entail preparations for this new way of transportation.

The huge gap between utopias and our existing world is evident. Many argue that our lives are closer to nightmares than they are to dreams. Any viable utopia designed today should engage the transportation problem from the outset. Perhaps the journey to our own utopia should start with developing new attitudes towards transportation. Before departure, though, it would be wise to have a quick glance at these earlier routes towards utopias. Perhaps one of them comes close to the place we have been dreaming of all along the way, and a whole new life awaits us there.

From Urban Cell to Global Hive
Maria del C. Vera and Shai Yeshayahu

[1] L. Mumford, **The City in History: Its Origins, Its Transformations, and Its Prospects** (Florida: Harcourt, Inc., 1961), 3

For centuries urbanity has shaped the milieu of the city—its central propulsion generates both material wealth and environmental scarcity. It is what led Lewis Mumford to the inconceivable question, 'Will the city disappear or will the whole planet turn into a vast urban hive?'[1]

Through layering processes, using world maps, and theories from emerging sociologists, economists, geographers, and political scientists, we envision the planet's survival as one vast urban world.

We are moving away from prototypical agendas based solely on material wealth, towards diversified realms founded on both site specificities and the economic wealth of the whole planet. In this context, general master plans executed by urbanists that sought strategies to define the city with buildings, bridges, highways, trains, airports, and water routes are blurred. Instead, increasing dependencies extending beyond local peripheries of richer and poorer cities are highlighted to demonstrate how urbanized and non-urbanized sites increasingly merge their interdependencies beyond distinguishable scopes.

The goal is to transcend beyond the essence of the twentieth-century city plan that has formed and informed current socio-economic agendas, and to make visible the invisible stratums that prompt urban flows, a discourse about intertwined links between urbanity and the economic wealth of the planet.

IMAGE OF URBANITY

Nearly five decades ago, in the introduction to *The City in History*, Mumford heralded an image of urbanity that stood out in contrast to conventional understandings regarding site, peripheries, and urban territories. Moving beyond political boundaries, it proposed a significant shift in scale and dependencies.

The persistence of a perceptual limitation based on political boundaries, however, is in part due to the modality that planners, architects, and landscapers

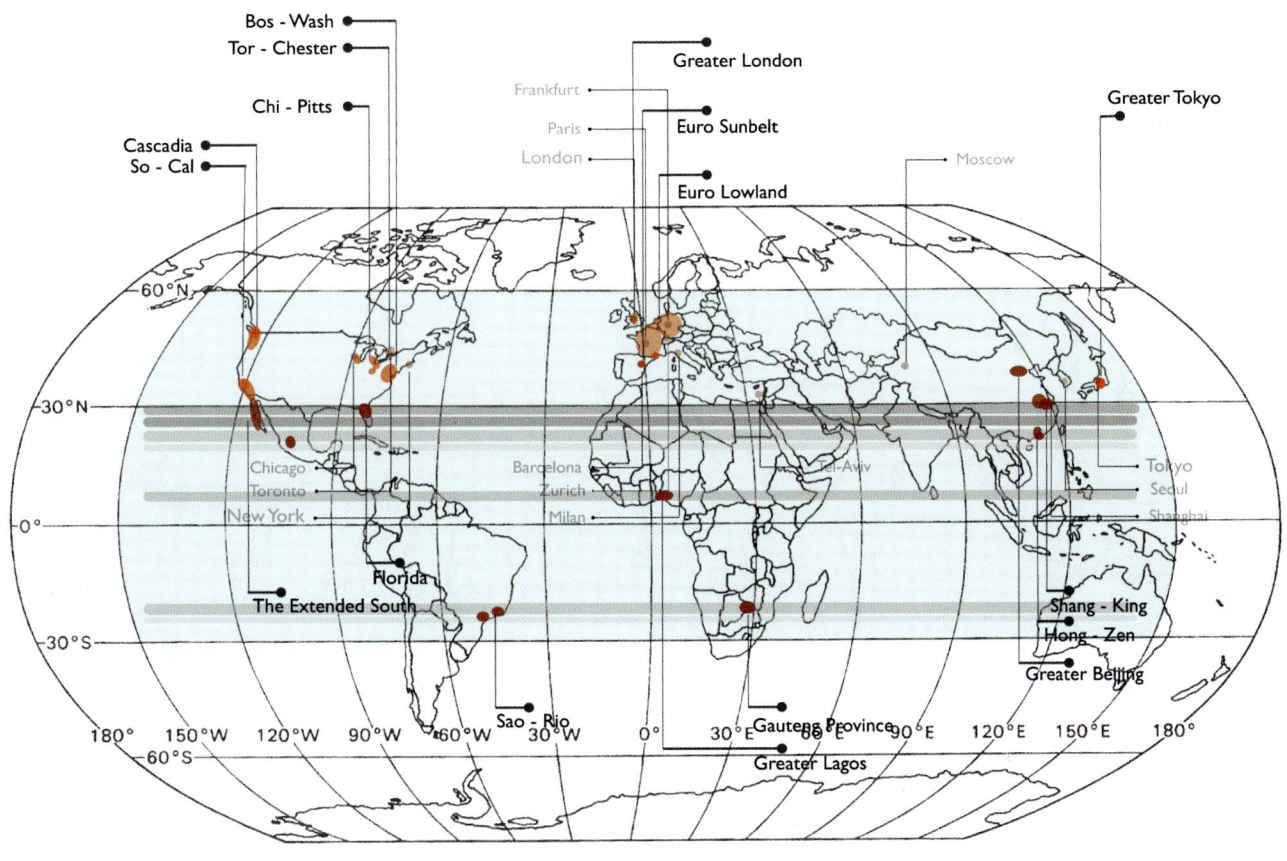

2 Mapping of the Wide Urban Belt demonstrates inequality in the distribution of global economical forces

utilize to define site, building, and city. The design-plan arena fixes relationships between form and place; site is rarely part of a larger vision capable of affecting and evolving the characteristics of planned space. Therefore, examining place as part of a larger system that learns, adapts, and transforms through time is an uncommon practice; and although scientists, geographers, and sociologists are able to explain the evolution of site, most of the built world is constructed under fixed pretences.[3]

[3] K. Easterling, Organization Space: landscape, highways, and houses in America (Cambridge: MIT Press, 1999)

In this regard, the differences of thought and processes between urbanists and other disciplines are palpable. Particularly, if we consider that forty-six years ago, as planners bypassed Mumford's inconceivable scale, the geographer Jean Gottmann recognized the whole northeastern region of the United States as a tightly interdependent area extending from Southern New Hampshire to Washington, D.C. He coined this specific socio-economic entity a megalopolis after the ancient Greek city known for its size, activities, and urban intensity. For Gottmann, the vision of a megalopolis trespassed population and organized units. He proposed that infrastructural, economic, and geographic conditions of the entire zone fostered interdependencies formed between the urban and nonurban qualities founded in cities, towns, farms, gardens, rivers, oceans, parks, and residue areas.

Thus, with the importance of evaluating urbanity beyond material activities, and riches, beyond the concept of the twentieth-century city known for its central core, repetition of forms, and fixed peripheries, lies the understanding that site is composed of multiple parts that are active and evolutionary. This is a critical shift that differs in concept from mankind's material pursuit to link places only through commercial routes that facilitated buying, selling, and the exchange of cultural goods. The recognition for an interlaced system that evolves from biochemical reactions influenced by living and nonliving matter ignites an understanding that the compositions of atmosphere, lithosphere, hydrosphere, and the forms we built are all part of one dynamic world.

INTERDEPENDENCIES

Today, Gottmann's theories regarding the socio-economic connectedness of a region are widely recognized; yet, his concept about interdependencies between urban and nonurban territories is not. For instance, sociologist Saskia Sassen and political scientist Richard Florida explain the links between cultural, political, and economic trends in the globalized era. Each has points of views that identify major international economic centers with their respective counterparts. Sassen, for example, coined the term Global City in reference to economic links found in specific financial markets like London, New York, and Tokyo, while Richard Florida refers to mega-corridors to argue that the significance of such urban clusters dwells in the bulk of work, talent, and wealth that their creative population provides. Despite their globalized understanding of material economies, Saasen and Florida are focused on the centrality of urbanity and its political territories.

Dependencies lie within all kinds of matter. A shift in thinking moves us away from political maps which articulate mankind's persistence to fragmentize site. A global understanding of one site, made of changing components, is

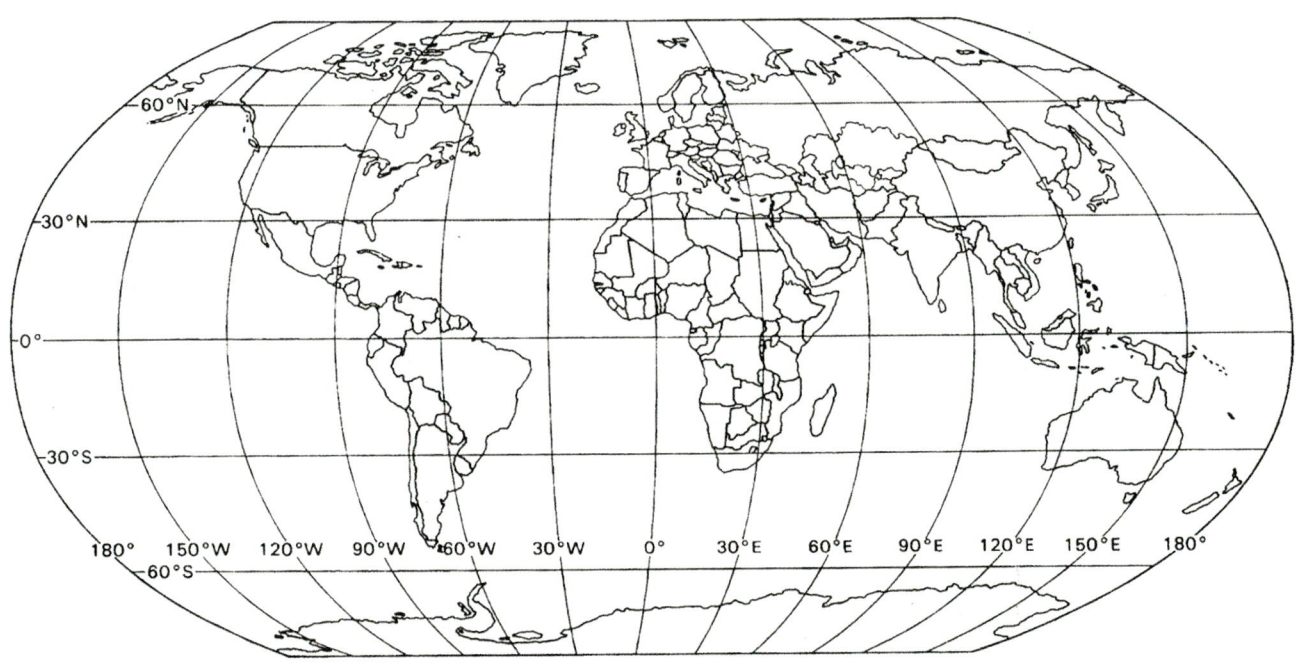

4 Mapping the World Wide Urban Hive

capable of developing new contexts that are not yet visible in the world of design. Gottmann's studies that sought to identify a complex interdependent mechanism between multiple cities within a specific region is yet to be recognized as a formula to identify a complex interdependent mechanism between multiple megalopoleis within one globalized site.

MAPPING PLACE

Urbanity has proven to be a challenge when socioeconomic hubs incrementally expand, the human population increases, and new territorial domains are conquered. Since its inception, the city continues to expand and grow into larger forms of urban scope. The geographic fundamentals defined in the megalopolis of the 1960s are today aggressive extensions and repetitions of habitable zones within the planet. They have reached a monumental scale that transcends individualized megalopoleis and forms one extended zone of urban dominance across the world.

Until now, thriving megalopoleis of the twentieth-century were independently recognized as BosWash, Sunbelt, Blue Banana, Cascadia, and so forth. Our mapping sequence assembles these interconnected regions according to their geodetic addresses and uncovers a visual circumferential strip of urban clusters located within a geodetic zone across the 30/60 degree latitudes, an urban sequence we call the 'Wide Urban Belt' (WUB).

WIDE URBAN BELT

The WUB is a vast urban zone that overpowers the rural areas as further intensifications of urbanity within the belt strengthen. In this regard, it denotes that a specific region houses humanity's thirst for material wealth, temperate climates, and developed networks. More importantly, as new and old megalopoleis are sited to their respective geodetic addresses, a mapped production of data about their site specificities and repetitions across the earth launches another discourse about urban hegemony. It signals a diluting condition occurring away from the WUB.

Scattered megalopoleis, rising to the surface, bring forth unaccountable repetitions of growth outside the WUB that reveal the unaccepted scale of the whole planet as one homogeneous globe. This unthinkable dispersal of urbanity demonstrates how human dominance thrives across the planet. It shows that other living forms are at risk of extinction. This emerging image of human hegemony shows the disequilibrium of parts caused by densities that incessantly replicate their form in different geographic terrains, regardless of environmental constraints; an urban trend that standardizes and morphs the composition of the planet. Thus, as megalopoleis spread beyond the WUB, an unrecognized system that we coined the 'World Wide Urban Hive' (WWUH) emerges.

WORLD WIDE URBAN HIVE

The WWUH is the unaccepted condition of urban scopes. It is the existence not only of clusters of megalopoleis that spread across the world, but of a fabricated

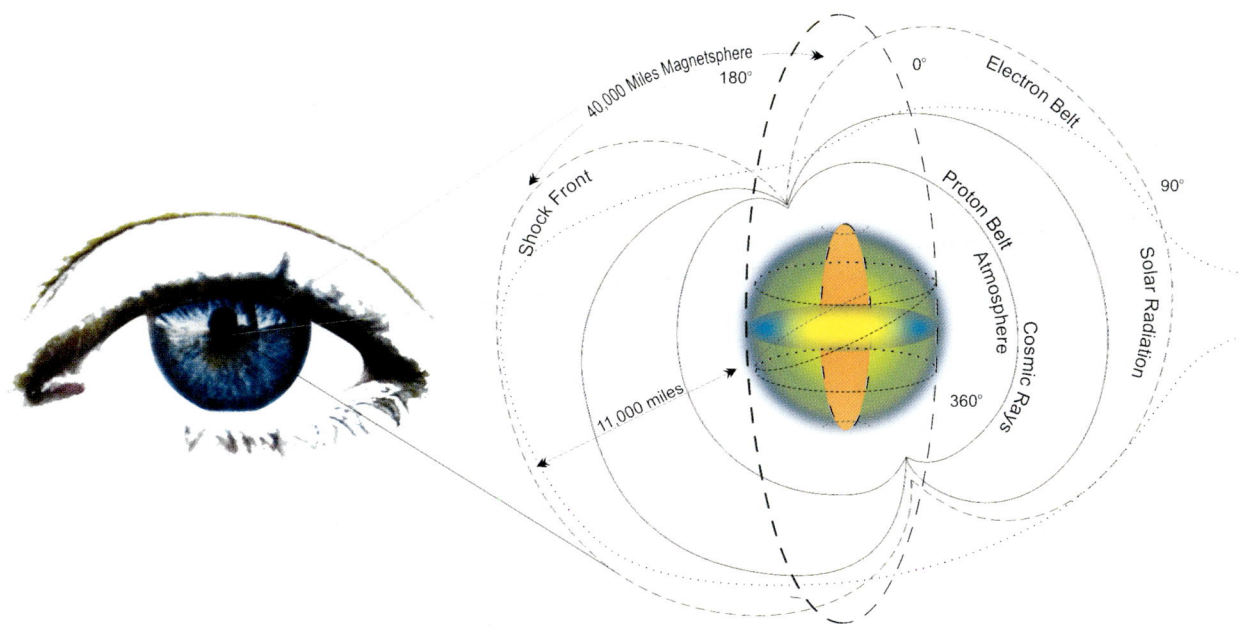

5 Envisioning the Noosphere

environment where the atmosphere, lithosphere, and hydrosphere can potentially become calibrated compositions synchronized by man. The WWUH transcends the notion that the biosphere is a self-generative system, and proposes that a man-made agenda formulates how changes in the environment occur. Thus, the question is no longer does the city disappear, but rather, can the whole planet survive as one vast urban hive?

To truly exploit the intelligence of the hive, we must recognize that urbanity prior to the twenty-first century flourished under the affluence of land and resources while the urbanity of this millennium reinvents, contracts, and constraints its growth under deficits of both. Urbanity and its built environment have exceeded their endless territorial extensions and entered a complex realm of interdependencies with all living and non-living matter. Thus, shifting operative modes from fields of unlimited resources to implosions of limited means, is similar to the survival skills displayed by a hive.

It is important that the WWUH grasps the hive's ability to adapt, group, and reinvent context in order to harbor resources and exist within changing frameworks. These techniques that maximize efficiencies and augment nutrients challenge conventional beliefs. Existing parameters and protocols for augmenting wealth will need to shift from political limitations and consumerism to reason. In this regard, the contradictions between current spaces of power and powerless spaces are interchangeable. Urban places recognized as part of the world economy and unrecognized places supporting the economy of the world are intertwined systems attempting to survive. The areas absent of light, population, and food are part of the environmental equation-as are the deserts, jungles, rainforest, and oceans. All places house qualities to augment the wealth of the planet and stabilize the atmosphere.

In the age of ubiquitous knowledge, informed design decisions are invaluable. Today, nourishing the biosphere is scientifically possible. Changing the composition of the biosphere to create resources would transform its chemical composition into something new that would no longer be the self-generative system, but a man-made production, the 'Noosphere', a term coined by Vernadsky. In Vernadsky's theory of how the Earth develops, the Noosphere is the third stage in a succession of phases of development of the earth, after the geosphere (inanimate matter) and the biosphere (biological life). Just as the emergence of life fundamentally transformed the geosphere, the emergence of human cognition fundamentally transformed the biosphere. In this theory, the principles of both life and cognition are the essential features of the earth's evolution, and must have been implicit in the earth all along. This is in contrast to Darwin's theory of natural selection, which looks at each individual species, rather than at its relationship to a subsuming principle.

NOOSPHERE

Like Vernadsky, we interpret the Noosphere to be a scientifically planned environment produced by mankind to reinvent resources for the whole planet. In this regard, the Noosphere is not a reproduction or mimicry. Instead it is a parameterization of data that hacks information from the existing ecological system. The data constantly reconditions the planet, as adaptations and reconfigurations of an ever-evolving system revises or revives, discredits, or validates the explorations of knowledge with informed actions. Urbanity will no longer be free to build its habitats at whim. Instead, we will work with an economy of means that is governed by evolution and the limitations of supply and demand. Scale, performance, and changes will be mandated by intelligent design solutions.

Initiatives concerned with issues of site specificities are springing up in the most populated places, like Lagos, Mexico City, Shanghai, Rio de Janeiro and China. Designers, engineers, and scientists are visualizing sites that focus on the performance of form and its relation to current environmental circumstances. For example, Columbia's Earth Institute under Cynthia Rosenzweig is creating a plan to redesign the harbor of greater New York City as a biosphere reserve and ARUP's team of designers and scientist proposes to integrate fauna, flora, housing, commercial strips, and high tech farming into what they call 'integrated urbanism'.[7]

These interventions are meshing local environmental constraints with human-built habitats. They are intelligent beginnings that may further engage with scientific agendas to spearhead a collection of data and studies that analyze successes or failures affecting the biochemical opus of the environment. These implementations would charge the beginning of a lifetime commitment to monitor and calibrate our environment.

NEW DESIGN FIELD

Mapping the trajectories of scale from city, to megalopolis, to urban hive, allows us to visualize a man-made world. The origins of a heterogeneously-composed environment governed by a natural selection of processes disappears. In its place, a highly monitored environment that requires uninterrupted maintenance emerges. A dynamic agenda replaces planning formats made of fixed elements in site.

This cognitive procedure is attentive to the fluctuations of evolutionary data and acts on its formation to provide a new design field for the survival of life. Thus, the world of tomorrow requires both vigilance and maintenance, as nothing is static, not even data. Successful solutions for the survival of the WWUH will require an optimistic point of view. Evolution will be design.

[7] Peter Head, ARUP. www.arup.com/sustainability/people.cfm?pageid=6008 (May 10 2007)

Genius Loci:
The Need for Urban Scenography
Adam Kolodziej

1 The African Tree

Facing Page
2 Sketch rendering of Zuma Rock

The complex and dramatic spatial construct we call 'the city' is an apogee of human civilization and its humanistic traditions. The art and culture of urban space formation is intricately related to and responds to the emotional complexity of human behavior. The city's spirit, its genius loci, affects the way individuals and communities coexist and interact. Genius loci strongly reflects the state of our society.

The current crisis of our 'practical' cities stems from the popular concept of the city as a machine. As it ignores life's emotional complexity it causes the disappearance of the city's genius loci. In today's city making, there is a strong need for what I call 'Urban Scenography'.

The art of scenography stems from the visualization of life's script, taking cues from history, cultural context and, most interestingly, from our emotional needs. In scenography, space is treated not only as a stage for our individual and collective dramas, but has become a living, dramatically charged character itself. The scenographic approach recognizes the city as an art form with its spatial drama unfolding over prolonged periods of time. The city space is treated as an indivisible, living organism. Urban scenography guides us through the time-space of the city; initiates our emotional link with its space and eventually reanimates and nourishes its genius loci.

GENIUS LOCI

The term genius loci originated in the early seventeenth century, but its roots are in Roman mythology where a genius loci referred to 'the presiding god or a guardian spirit' of a place. In Latin, it literally means 'spirit of the place'. In contemporary usage, it has a wider sense of the prevailing character of a location and usually

3 Ruins of the Greco-Roman and Persian metropolis of Palmyra

4 Genius loci of the city of Wurzburg, Germany after Balthasar Neumann in 1723

5 Wenceslas Square in Prague, after Vincenc Morstadt in 1835

refers to its distinctive atmosphere. Several architects of the 1970s and the 1980s recognized its importance while promoting phenomenology; a design current based on the physical scale and haptic experience of building materials and their sensory properties.

Genius loci expresses our emotional relationships with space. It is an aggregate of our individual memories and dramas within the context of the city. The city's own drama, in turn, is visually reflected in its physical character and embraces the whole of urban life. The city has been created as a narrative environment with its functional aspect as secondary. Its function is based upon necessities but, more importantly, it has the power to satisfy the need of an individual to develop a very personal story.

The experience of genius loci predates the birth of the city. It started millennia ago with our amazement at nature's creations; the climate, topography, waters, transient light, and all the wonders that humans are drawn to. Nature's formations inspired the proto-elements of the early city: the path, the gate, and the domineering verticality of the stronghold. Stimulated by nature's emotive qualities, man's first emotions were shared when people met and exchanged their stories. Then they exchanged goods. Soon there was a need for a recognizable place. A safe place, where the energy of the Earth materialized in a unique rocky outcrop, the edge of the plateau with a wide view, a peninsula or an island. Then, with time, the city was born, the living body of man-made space. It developed and matured slowly around a few quintessential elements: the stronghold as a governing, self controlling 'head'; the temple as an emotional, spiritual 'heart'; the market space as a socially engaging and fulfilling 'stomach'; all supported and linked by a cardiovascular system of arteries within areas of human habitation. Having evolved as a manifestation of nature and human spirit, the city is the portrait of its society. It expresses its culture and its humanism. Like a theatre it reflects our life while enriching and elevating our emotions above our practical, biological needs. The starting point for a city was a story, a legend loaded with meanings and emotions to stimulate our imagination and to inspire our creativity in shaping the drama of space. It strengthened our ability to materialize our dreams.

EXPERIENCING GENIUS LOCI

The imposing and mysterious monolith of Zuma Rock is located off the main road that goes north from the capital Abuja to Kaduna, at the exact geographical centre of Nigeria. It is a landmark that largely defines the area. Local beliefs forbid climbing it and its powerful juju (energy) is claimed to stem from inhabiting gods and spirits. It is the Mount Olympus of the West African tribes and both predominantly Christian Yoruba and Muslim Hausa respect its genius loci.

In the shadow of the Zuma rock the local community gathers and exchanges stories. They make collective decisions. One day they started a small settlement; soon they will create a city, as the Greeks did at the foot of the Acropolis, some 2,500 years ago.[2]

The institution of the African Tree is very prominent within a typical village's environment. Beginning as merely a noticeable landmark, this tree becomes the focal point for a variety of activities. It develops into the community's nursing and public school, its university, its theatre and its Heritage Board. As its presence assures the continuation of community's universal values it becomes the symbol of settlement's genius loci.¹

The ruins of the Greco-Roman and Persian metropolis of Palmyra (present day Syria) provide another example of the urban environment with its genius loci still intact. The crest of the nearby hill inspired Arabs in the sixth century to transform it into the fortress. Both the remaining city gate and the fortress create dramatic visual nodes that define the quintessence of polis/urbs/city.³

The genius loci of the city of Wurzburg, Germany was portrayed by Balthasar Neumann in 1723. The city was presented as a dramatic character on life's stage. Its appearance marks the zenith of its society's cultural, social, and economic advancement. It is an indivisible and emotive spatial construct. Its scenography was created both consciously and incidentally by its citizens and has been enriched by the passage of time. It becomes an important character in the drama of individual and community life. The city, as presented here with outmost reverence and respect, becomes the portrait of its creator: the enlightened and cultured society.⁴

6 Paris in 1858, after a wood-engraving of 1858

Wenceslas Square in Prague, as seen by Vincenc Morstadt in 1835 is the apotheosis of the joys of city life. It is an urban spectacle that is the result of eight centuries of cohesive development of a stable urban community. Time was given the chance to enrich the space with its patina.⁵

Just twenty years later, in 1858, another great European city, Paris, was touched by the 'grand scheme'. Its urban structure and its medieval genius loci was disregarded and mutilated. Hundreds of years of time patina were erased. It was an act of urban vandalism in the name of 'new values'. It was like burning the books our illiteracy prevents us to read.⁶

Genius loci is experienced in layers of space-time. The first layer appears as we travel from the paradise of nature toward the miracle of the city. Approaching the city one is full of anticipation and hope. We always search for a vantage point to appreciate it in its entirety. We approach its defined outer shape, its intriguing skyline with the same thrill as entering the opera theatre lobby. At this point, the city does not reveal its script.⁷

7 Approaching the city

Then opening the outer shell like a theatre curtain comes a bridge, a gate, and an avenue. There is the dramatic sensation of opening a book. Page after page the urban script unfolds, saturating our senses with ever-changing chiaroscuro and textures. We are constantly gazed upon by the multitude of details, the means of previous generations to communicate with us. We are able to read the meaning of some and appreciate the intensity of others.⁸

The path leads us through alternating narrow and wide spaces, zones of light and shadow that alternately hide and reveal the rhythm of vertical elements. We are introduced to the characters of this urban drama and we just begin to recognize their language. Other spectators-citizens surround us. Each of us experience this urban drama through the prism of our own script. Each of us is at a different level of engagement and understanding. We find the length of the

8 Opening the outer shell like a theatre curtain comes a bridge

Genius Loci: The Need for Urban Scenography | 70

9 Multilayered composite of a one thousand years old urban architectural entity

10 Portable theatre of the Krakow Crib

Facing Page
11 From new heights we can see the next node of urban space. The square allows us to make the choice of new direction.

path acceptable and the height of the walls not intimidating. Friendly, well-worn pavement assures us that many before walked here and survived. Our every step changes our framing for the ever-present sky, our constant link with nature. Side paths and occasional openings allow us to penetrate into this urban script and slow down. There is the constant change of proportions, always balanced. Scale-defining details are combined into phrases of architectural elements, paragraphs of complimenting styles, and the volume of urban space.

A main path, meandering or relatively straight, leads our curiosity towards a dominant, vertical structure. Once we reach it, it persuades us to slow down, stop, and look up. The vertical element elevates our attitude and provokes our imagination to fly.

Now we are high above the main square, overseeing the communal, open space. The phenomenon of so-called 'empty space' is brimming with constantly rewritten scripts and dramas. It is a space of condensation and dispersion. Its eternal existence questions the importance of the city's physicality. Is this empty space the city itself? Walking toward it, we are walking into the city. Leaving it, we go away from the city. The city is the aggregate of our individual activities, the highest density of which occurs within this empty/full space of the main square. Its presence proves the importance of the space without definite program or singular purpose: the importance of allowing and creating spaces for spontaneous human interaction. There are several paths leading to and from the main square. They link us with sacred spaces, governing centers and some re-link us with nature.

From new heights we can see the next dramatic, dominant node of urban space. The square allows us to make the choice of new direction.[11]

A new path emerges and a new story unfolds.

At one point we reach the complex, yet harmonious, multilayered composite of a 1,000 year old urban/architectural entity. It was created by generations and governed by a respect for what has come before.[9]

Enchantment with tradition keeps genius loci alive. Every matured urban community recognizes the City as a stage for life's theatre and appreciates its scenographic artifact. The architectural legend and the visual poetry of the portable theatre of the Krakow Crib is individually created by citizens as a spontaneous response to their enchantment with the real. They use the scenographic features of the actual cityscape as inspiration for their paper and tinfoil constructs.[10]

DILEMMA OF THE MODERN CITY

There is a famous phrase from Le Corbusier: 'Man walks in a straight line because he has a goal and knows where he is going'. As a young man I followed this unwavering straightforwardness. Then I realized, with relief, that I have never seen a natural river flow in a straight line. I also realized that my goals are constantly shifting and are often foggy, delightfully so.

One can almost forget that Le Corbusier was a significant artist the moment one encounters his urban schemes.[12] Propelled by certain doctrines he decided to hide all the riches of social complexity within a monoculture of abstractly neutral boxes. His act of urban intolerance for Algiers, his acts of creative rage for

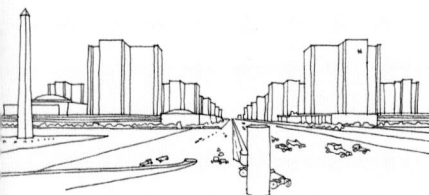

12 The Modern City, after Le Corbusier

13 Venice, genius loci

14 The emotive space of memories

Facing Page
15 Venice, genius loci
All images and photographs within this essay by Adam Kolodziej unless otherwise indicated

Marseille and for Paris are petrifying. His political and social naiveté, his arrogance and his focus on an object, blinded him into abandoning both the process of creating and the process of experiencing the city. Within his vast open spaces there is not an inch for the human individual. Today, we still feel and suffer the aftershocks of his acts of urban tyranny.

What we call a modern city is not a city I know and respect. It is yet another mass product: intellectual, efficient, practical and, yes, lifeless. An abstract spatial construct, a three-dimensional financial chart hypocritically claiming to provide 'spaces for everybody' but in reality providing spaces for nobody. Its visual language constantly promises us freedom to reveal and share our individual scripts and dramas but in fact deprives us of that very essential right. The current urban crisis stems also from the popular concept of the city as a machine. The Machine fears the passage of time. But we, humans, do age with every passing second and we like our city to accompany us, with grace, in our journey through time.

CREATING GENIUS LOCI: AN URBAN SCENOGRAPHER'S RECOMMENDATION

- Recognize the city as a dramatic art form.
- Acknowledge culture as a city forming force.
- Recognize society's aesthetic sensitivity.
- Create urban emotive space.
- Stimulate the individual and communal memories of the urban emotive space.
- Think script, not program. Define urban script. Focus on the narrative quality of space.
- Think character, not form.
- Appreciate the visual potential of the natural site.
- Accept the importance of the legend, related to the site.
- Provide and protect the natural flow and continuum of space.
- Develop the sequence and impact of dramatic spatial nodes.
- Appreciate the patina of time.

EPILOGUE

Venice's genius loci is not necessarily in the golden domes of St. Mark's basilica. It is in its ever-changing, turbulent, water-giving skies. It is measured by the pulse of the Lagoon's water. It is about the superhuman effort of transporting millions of oak tree trunks down the Veneto rivers and testing them against oscillating water levels, humidity, time, and, yes, decay. It is about 1,000 years of inspired and inspiring urban drama.

It projects itself through the script of human life, played within the drama of the space.[13] Even the most sublime form and light is not enough to create the genius loci.[14] Genius loci is the sum of our individual memories within the context of the emotive space. Memories as quiet and insignificant as a speck of charcoal dust or as powerful and vast as the Universe.

Towards Constructive Dialogue: Real-Time Visualization and Geographic Information Systems

Thomas Seebohm and John Danahy

1 Participatory Urban Design with three-screen immersive display, Centre for Landscape Research

Facing Page
2 Virtual 3D urban, real-time model of the University of Toronto campus

Citizens are no longer content to consume information in public information meetings concerning future urban development scenarios for their cities. Contemporary urban design and planning increasingly requires visual dialogue and negotiation supported by appropriate visual tools, namely three dimensional visualization in real-time linked to related abstract information. The dramatic reductions in cost of hardware that have brought virtual reality simulations from the laboratory to the laptop are beginning to make appropriate visual tools available for effective participatory urban planning and design. Still somewhat of a hurdle is the availability of software that is inexpensive, that is accessible to a broad range of people in addition to government bodies, and that supports debate of the specific issues involved in participatory urban design and planning.

The evolution of visual media is thus adding a layer of negotiation to both the consumption and crafting of images for urban decision-making. Real-time immersive visualization offers the ability to analyze and debate the merits of design that affect the shared landscapes of Canada's cities. Moreover, real-time visualization presents a potential means of overcoming the conventional public consultation model where the designer, developer, and government bodies are all placed in privileged roles, controlling and editing information that is presented for public feedback.[1] The norm in current public information meetings is one where two-dimensional plans and marketing renderings are presented and explained in professional language. Seldom do professionals talking about future development show people what their words and plans mean in terms of relevant eye level experience, how the experience will change through time, and how this experience relates to relevant urban statistics. Real-time visualization

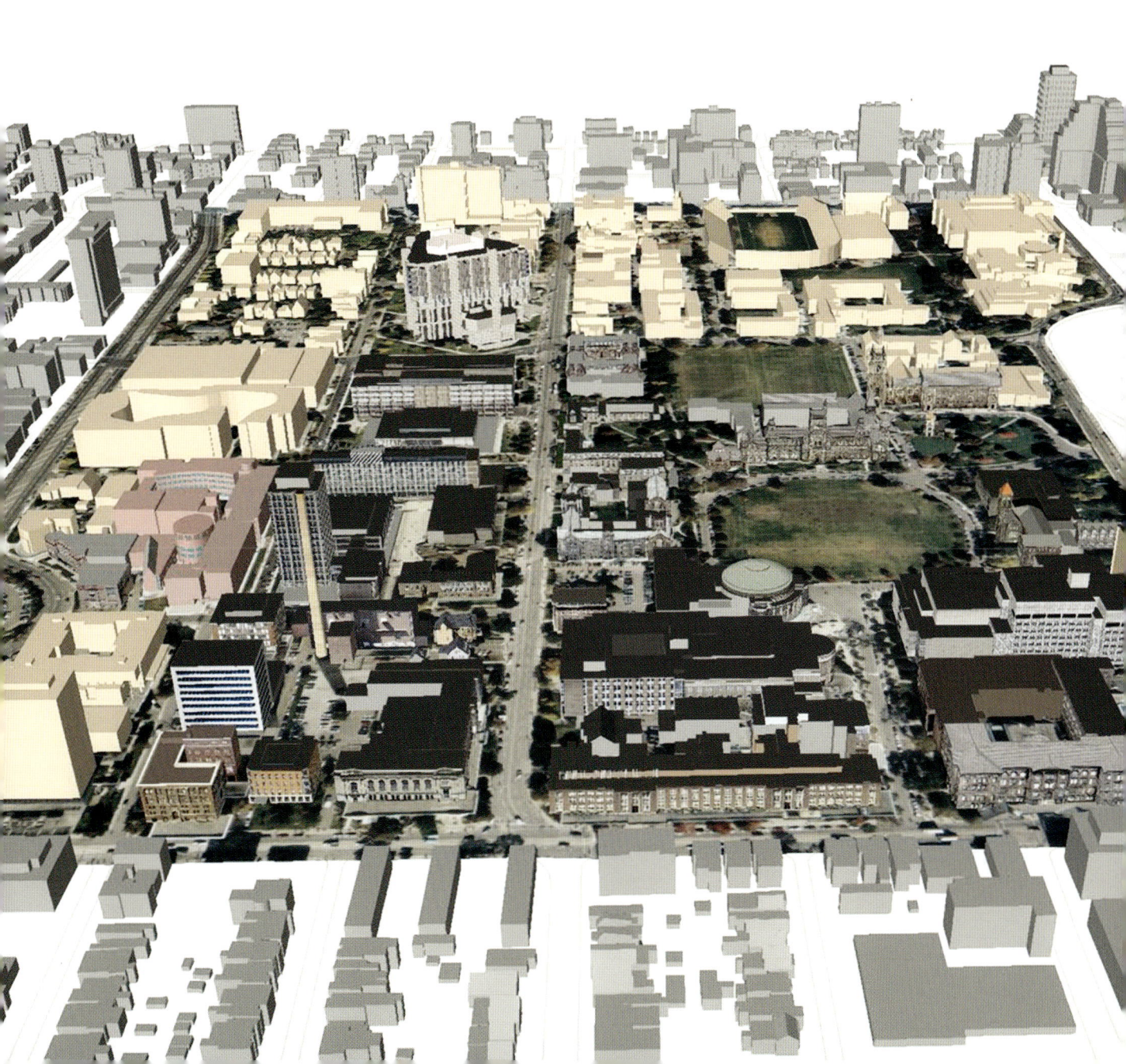

3 Virtual 3D urban, real-time model of downtown Kitchener, King Street looking west

4 OrbisRT is being developed by Rodney Hoinkes by building on an earlier version, NeoPD, developed at the University of Waterloo by Kevin Moule with software components by Michael McCool and in collaboration with the authors, Rodney Hoinkes and Pierre Côté of Laval University.

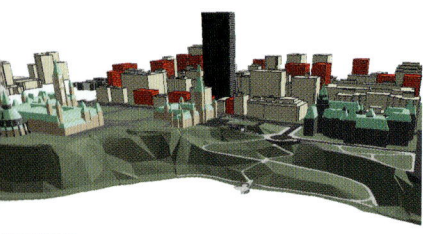

5 Economic analysis of office space in downtown Ottawa (1994)

makes dialogue possible because it is not exclusively a one-way presentation to people conveying only the expertise and giftedness of the professional. The fundamental difference using a real-time media is that one can interrogate, look for oneself and even re-propose and negotiate using the images of the virtual model. Dialogue becomes possible.

Figures 2 and 3 show still images of virtual, 3D urban models of the University of Toronto campus and King Street in downtown Kitchener, respectively. The images were captured from the screens of real-time displays created with collaborative viewing software called Poetic Dimensions developed by Rodney Hoinkes with John Danahy. The virtual urban models displayed by this software are usually as photorealistic as currently possible to allow viewers to experience as convincingly as possible what a future urban environment will be like. Sometimes, however, we create massing models without photorealism when providing a context for a virtual urban model, as in Figure 2, where a photorealistic model of the campus is surrounded by a context consisting of buildings shown as masses only (massing models show the shape of buildings without showing details such as windows).

Equally important to the level of detail provided by the virtual models is the fact that they are displayed in real time. This means that one can visualize the model by moving through virtual space as if one was walking through real, three-dimensional space at one's own pace without being constrained by predetermined views.

Allowing people to see for themselves requires that the software for viewing and the data comprising the 3D urban models is freely available to municipal governments as well as the public. The first objective is being fulfilled by the development of a completely new, open source version of the collaborative viewing software to be called OrbisRT. By making the software open source, both the software and the source code will be freely available.[4]

While we are helping the objective of freely available software, cities will have to step forward to create and make their 3D models freely available. The world is on the cusp of a great deal of interest in 3D urban visualization and related software developments. In the long run we may not need to develop our own software for real-time urban visualization, although there will likely still be a need for special utilities relating to urban development.

For knowledgeable public participation in planning, the real-time visual information of the 3D urban models must be complemented with abstract information related to the proposed development being viewed. Associated abstract information such as the persons per hectare, the rentable floor area, economic impact and traffic impact are essential for understanding the full implications of proposed urban development. Figures 5 and 6 show early attempts to link abstract information to 3D visual models. Figure 5 shows an economic analysis of office space in downtown Ottawa with information such as gross and net floor areas, while Figure 6 shows similar information for a study of the King Street–Spadina Avenue area in downtown Toronto. More recently, information from Geographic Information Systems (GIS) has been linked directly to the display of three-dimensional urban massing models using special software

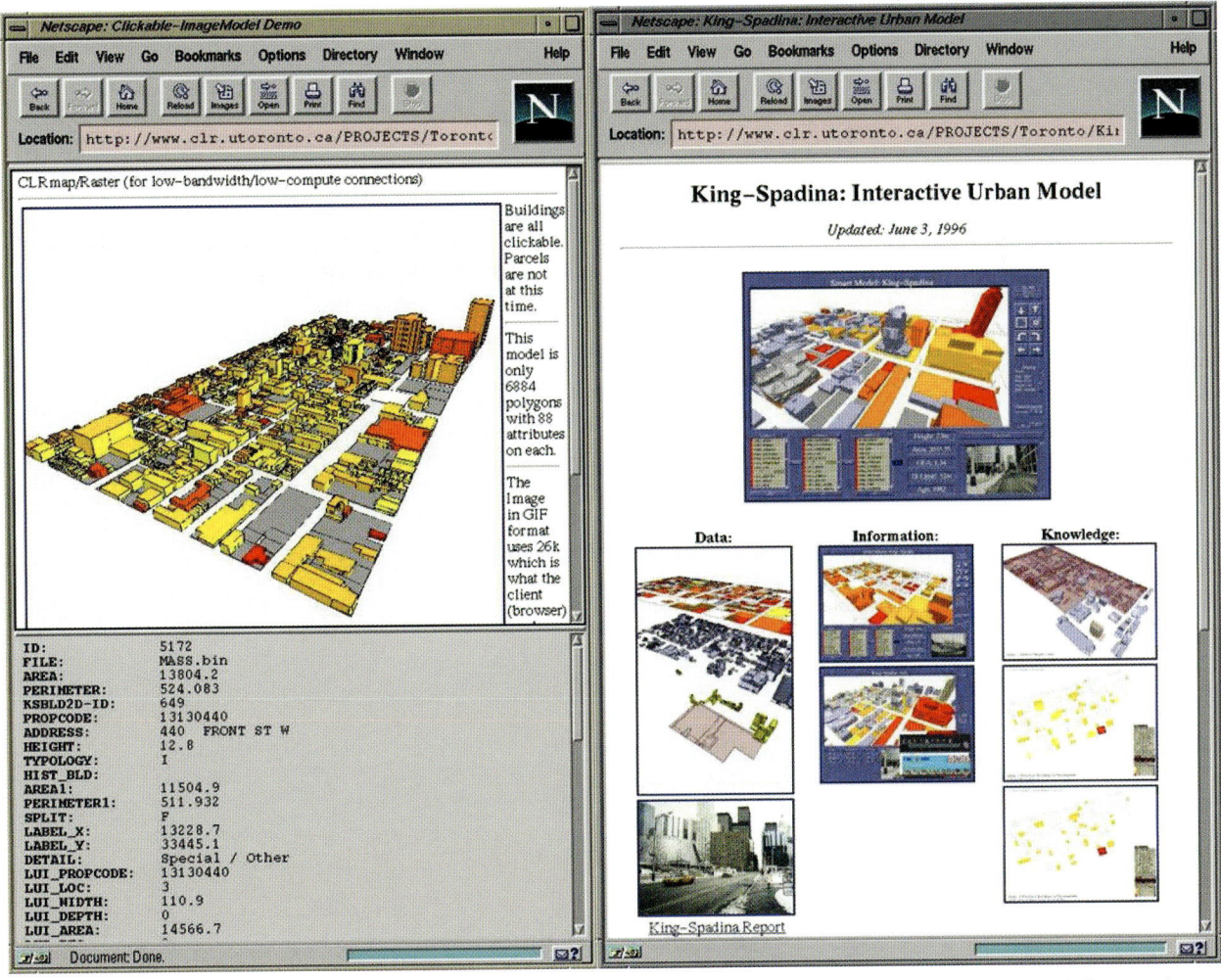

6 Economic analysis of office space in the King Street-Spadina Avenue area of Toronto (1996)

[7] E. Allen, 'INDEX: Software for Community Indicators', **Planning Support Systems: Integrating Geographic Information Systems Models and Visualization Tools**, R. Brail (ed.) (Redlands: Rutgers University Centre for Urban Policy Research and ESRI Press, June 2000), 229-261

[8] Spiro Kostof, 'Urbanism and Polity: Medieval Siena in Context', **International Library for Architecture and Urban Design**, Yearbook, (Florence: Sansoni Editore, 1982), 66-73

[9] J. Kaliski, 'Democracy Takes Command', **Havard Design Magazine** (Spring/Summer 2005), 20-26

such as the INDEX software.[7] Linking GIS systems with collaborative real-time, urban visualization is a promising area of research.

PUBLIC PROCESS IMPROVES OUTCOMES

It is often believed that those picturesque Italian hill towns in Tuscany, such as Siena, with their curving streets and graceful public squares developed haphazardly, largely influenced by the contours of the terrain. On the contrary, Spiro Kostof has shown that the development of these cities was the result of intense public debate and negotiation.[8] More recent experience in Los Angeles suggests that knowledgeable public participation always improves outcomes over what would have resulted, if the form of future development had been left in the hands of specialists. For such public involvement to be successful there should be an infrastructure to support it. In Los Angeles this has taken the form of funded local community councils. When the public becomes involved with appropriate access to information they become experts themselves and no longer require planners and urban designers to advocate good urban design principles. What a knowledgeable public needs, according to Kaliski, is planners and urban designers who can complement the knowledge of the citizens by guiding the planning process with public participation and by showing the public the visual consequences of their desires in terms of buildable proposals and related impacts in quantitative terms. This is where there is a great need, writes Kaliski, for software tools to allow citizens to visualize these buildable proposals and simultaneously view the quantitative impacts at economic, social, infrastructural (including transportation), and environmental levels.[9]

Perhaps the most stunning impact that visualization has had on public participation actually occurred just before computers came to be commonly used in architecture and planning offices. This was the case of the proposed development of the Mission Bay District in South San Francisco in 1984.

10 Mission Bay Proposal for San Francisco as simulated at the Berkeley Environmental Simulation Laboratory

Peter Bosselman and collaborators at the Environmental Simulation Lab at UC Berkeley had developed a large physical model of San Francisco that one could examine as if one was immersed in the real city looking at it from various vantage points. Figure 10 shows the view from south Market Street towards the bay and Mission Bay. On the left are the tall buildings of the existing downtown and on the right the towers of the Mission Bay proposal. It became instantly clear to everyone that the proposal would dramatically compete with the existing downtown. This was totally unacceptable to all concerned with the result that ultimately a low-rise, mixed-use development in the best sense of a livable, walkable, urban fabric was recently built. As an aside, it should also be noted that the effect of visualizing this development was so powerful that visualization was not used in the Bay Area in the years that followed.[11] While this was unfortunate, it does prove the power of visualization. Visualization with real-time, near photorealistic models improves upon a physical model because the imagery in the near visual field is more convincing and because one does not have to rely on views created by others.

11 Peter Bosselman, **Representation of Places** (Berkeley: University of California Press, 1998)

DIFFERENT ROLES OF REAL-TIME, 3D URBAN VISUALIZATION IN THE PLANNING PROCESS

When planning completely new future development, revitalization or densification of cities, it becomes clear that it is not enough to have a master plan represented by two-dimensional maps of zoning districts, zoning regulations supplemented by urban design guidelines, and a written strategic plan. What is needed is a stimulating vision in three dimensions of what the future city or part thereof is to look like. The City of Helsinki has been taking this approach for many years whenever it has moved to develop a new section of the city by initiating an urban design competition for the overall visual form of that section of the city coupled

12 Ian Chodikoff, 'A Tale of Two Cities', Canadian Architect (52, 4, 2007), 43

13 Ottawa ceremonial route study (1988)

14 Pedestrian-friendly proposal for Gaukel Street at the bus transit terminal in Kitchener. (Real-time image modified in PhotoShop, 2004)

15 Landscape proposal for the entrance to Victoria Park, Kitchener (2004)

with a strategic plan. Recently the planning director of the City of Vancouver, Brent Toderian, and the director of urban design of the City of Toronto, Robert Freedman, both emphasized the need for a physical vision of the city.[12] Moreover, they felt that this vision should be shaped by the cities themselves through a culture that promotes good design and public discussion.

The primary purpose of real-time 3D urban visualization is for the public to be able to participate in the development of that vision by being able to see the physical form of alternate visions. Once the overall vision has been accepted, 3D real-time urban visualization can be used to develop more detailed proposals over a wide range of applications. For example, a study of height and view corridors was investigated in the Ottawa Height Control study in 1994.[16] Another application is the detailed study of streetscape design including vegetation, street furniture, lighting, and paving. A pioneering study of this kind, long before it became economical to do this on desktop computers, was the Ottawa ceremonial route study of 1988.[13] A more recent example is an image of a proposal for revisions to Gaukel Street in Kitchener to make it more pedestrian friendly.[14] Even park design is within the realm of possibility as shown by the study of a new entrance for Victoria Park in Kitchener with detailed representation of trees and planting beds.[15] One of the most important uses of real time models is to assess future urban development either in terms of individual buildings,[17] or in terms of larger assemblages of buildings and the spaces they frame. To ensure that a physical urban vision is implemented, there must also be height and massing regulations and urban design regulations to ensure that the desired physical vision is realized. Real-time visualization can be used to check that all possible interpretations of the regulations meet the intent of the urban vision embodied in the regulations.

HOW RELIABLE IS URBAN VISUALIZATION?

Artistic impressions of what a proposed urban development will look like are just that: impressions—whether they are done manually or by digital means. 3D urban models can be geo-referenced, consisting of accurate terrain models based on surveys (usually to one half metre accuracy) and digital line drawings of street and building footprints to the same accuracy. Figure 19 shows the overall process whereby three layers of Geographic Information System (GIS) data are superimposed: an ortho air photo of the site with a resolution of about fifteen centimeters per pixel, a digital terrain model, and a layer with accurate street and sidewalk edges and building footprints. Buildings are created from simple geometry based on the building footprints and field information including building heights measured with a laser range finder. Occasionally, photogrammetry methods are used to model buildings directly from digital photos. Cropped and rectified photos of the building elevations are texture mapped to the surfaces of the simple geometry of the building. Finally, the buildings are positioned in three-dimensional space using 3D points (x,y,z coordinate points) that we produce from the GIS data.

Once good model data is available, one needs a way to simulate the interaction of the visual field with the virtual data model and do it in a way that our eyes are adapted to sense and our mind is organized to perceive.[18] Our visual system has two fundamental components: foveal and peripheral vision. The foveal system allows us to sample the visual field in fine detail and the peripheral system provides

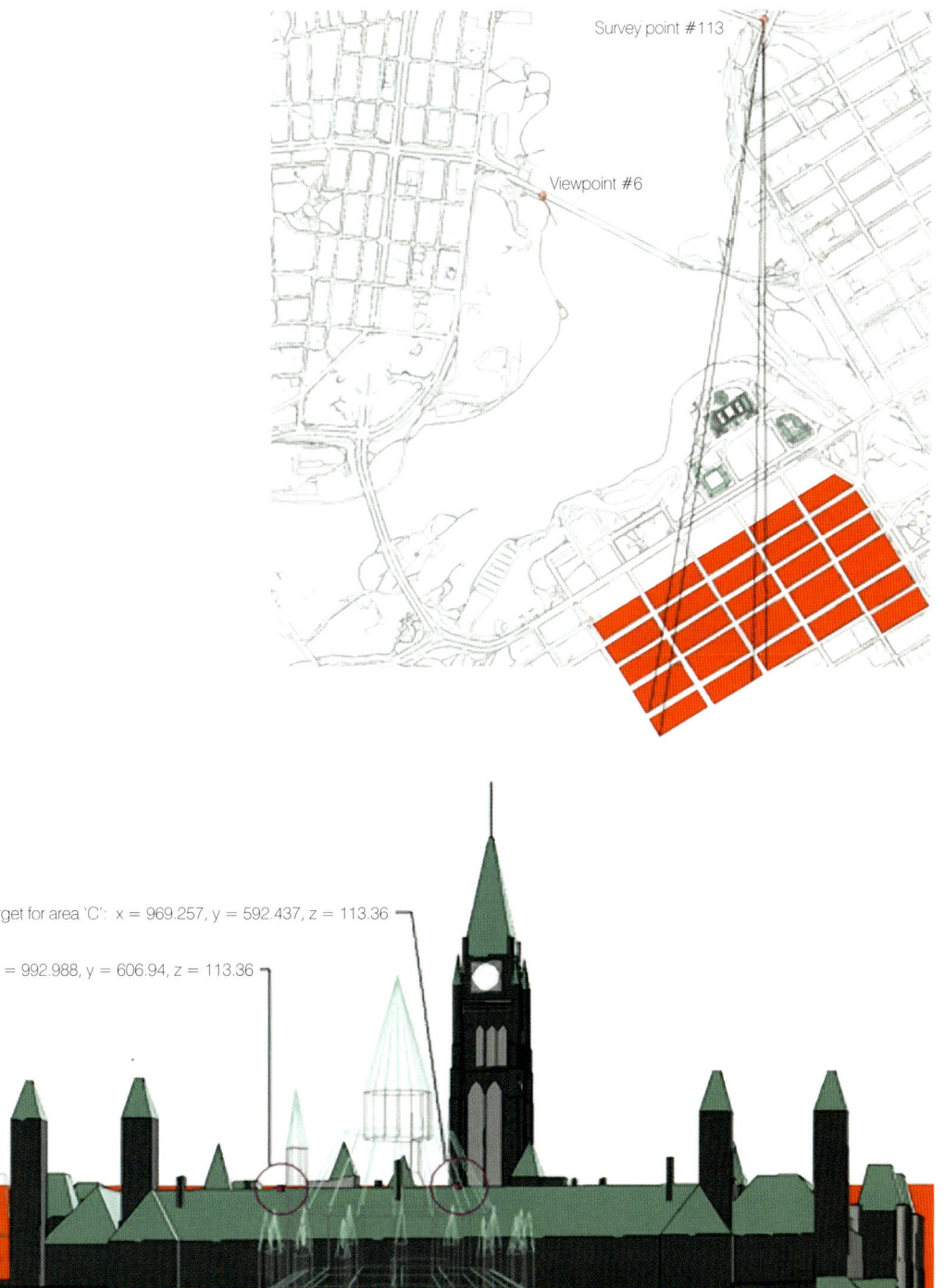

16 Ottawa height control study (1994)

17 Schematic proposal for a new public library in downtown Kitchener (2004)

18 John Danahy, 'Dynamic Immersive Visual Dialogue', **The Real and the Virtual World of Planning**, M. Koll-Schretzenmayr, M. Keiner, and G. Nussbaumer, eds. (Berlin, Heidelberg: Springer-Verlag, 2003)

us with our contextual spatial understanding of the visual field. The first generation of computer graphics automated the process of making single perspective drawings and has advanced to include greater degrees of photo and optical realism. Images on a single computer screen support foveal vision which has a narrow field of view and high detail. Foveal vision focuses mental attention on single objects. Real-time computer graphics make it possible to freely look and move around sampling objects with foveal vision. The addition of immersive visualization with a panoramic display allows extension of the field of view and use of peripheral vision to understand space and movement through a space. Peripheral vision is essential to obtain a balanced understanding of space that is not biased by the limited field of view of foveal vision. Peripheral vision is adapted to provide people with spatial context and does not introduce the distortion created by single images corresponding to a particular focal length of a camera or cone of vision of a computer generated image. Today's low cost, immersive real-time visualization tools are affordable and capable of representing the most fundamental dimensions of human vision that underpin design thinking and dialogue.

REGULATING THE USE OF URBAN VISUALIZATION

All parties involved in participatory urban planning and design using 3D urban visualization should have the assurance that what they are looking at is an accurate portrayal of the issues under consideration. What process can provide this assurance and how can this be regulated? To provide this assurance it is essential that anyone can reproduce the images being shown in a participatory session provided they have a copy of the data, the software, and a visualization computer of the same specification. Consistent reproduction is possible because the systematic nature of real-time computer images is based on standardized, pier-reviewed algorithms for visualization. By contrast, hand-made imagery such as an artist's sketch or conventional advertising rendering is not reproducible by others.

In the sense of consistent reproduction, this real-time visualization meets the scientific test that others should be able to replicate a given set of results if they question another person's findings. This basic property allows participants in a process to see for themselves and to precisely question the images put before them. Our experience shows that in case studies where real-time visualization is available to all participants, a process of self regulation and peer review helps to ensure and satisfy participants that what they are looking at is an accurate portrayal of the issue under study. Where greater precision is required or where consistency from decision to decision is important, then the data and the visualization parameters can be checked and verified by a third party expert (from fields such as surveying, photogrammetry, geomatics) or by a visualization expert if the application parameters used to make an image require objective certainty. In the case of development approvals, it is a relatively straight forward process to define a specification for submission materials. As the culture of use expands we may see a level of certification appear. For instance, in the City of Ottawa where the tools have been used to establish height controls, the regulating elements in the visualization were surveyed and newly completed buildings must supply a surveyor's certificate that confirms the 'as-built' height of the building.

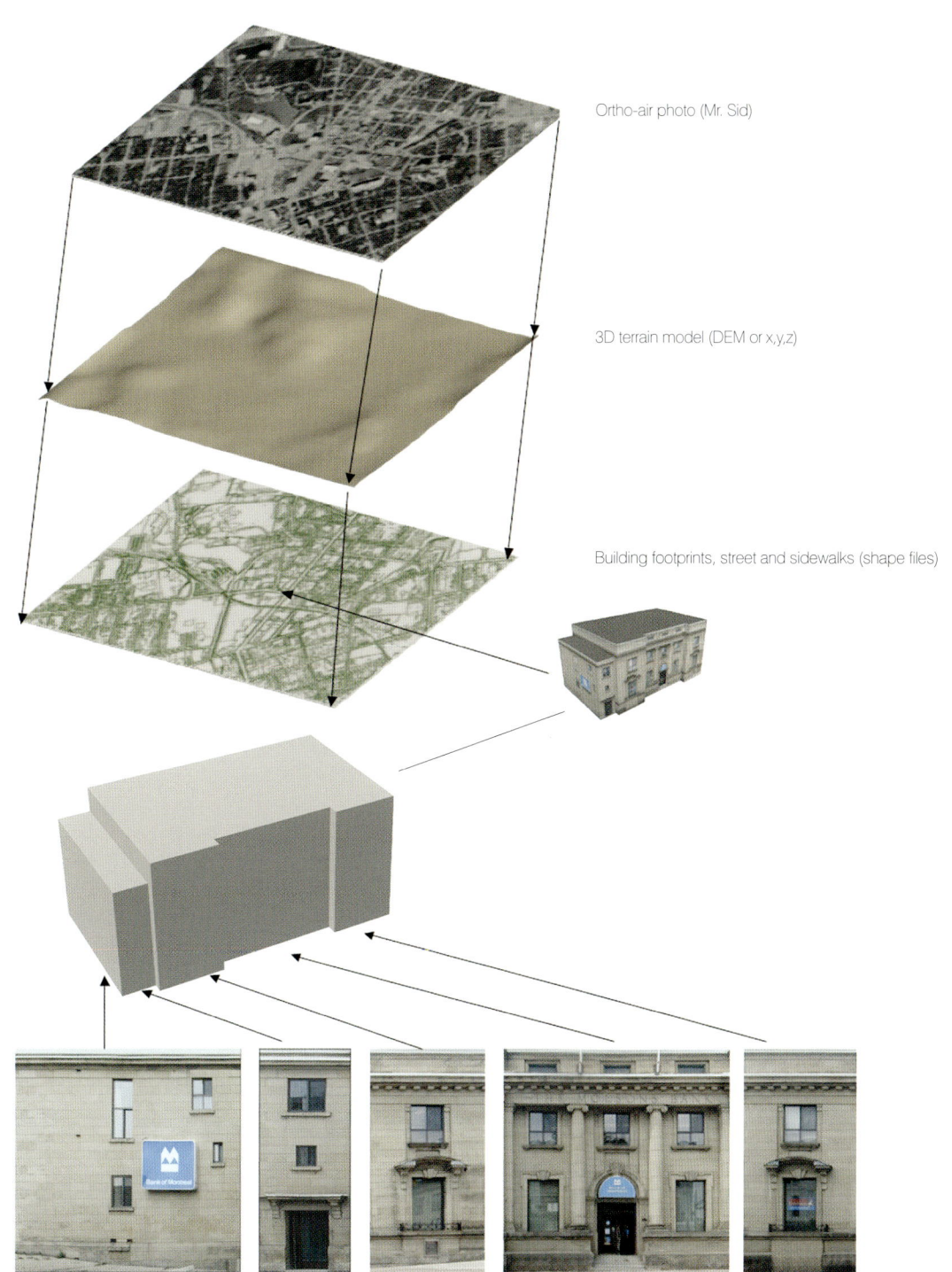

19 Creating accurate geo-referenced 3D urban virtual models

[20] A. Hamilton, N. Trodd, X. Zhang, T. Fernando and K. Watson, 'Learning through visual systems to enhance the urban planning process', **Env. and Plan. B.** (28, 2001), 833-845

Some cities use 3D virtual models as part of the planning process and thereby regulate the use of these technologies. Among these cities is Edinburgh, that requires 3D models for any new proposals in the old town.[20] London has an extensive 3D urban model, parts of which are photorealistic. The London model is similar in quality to the Edinburgh model. Requiring the submission of 3D models of proposals for insertion into a 3D virtual model of a city in order to study the fit with the context sets a standard for the use of the models. When a city does so, however, it must also set standards for the submission of the virtual models such as the file formats, the level of detail, the construction of the models in terms of cleanliness, surface normals, texture file resolution, and formats, among others.

ADOPTION OF REAL-TIME, 3D URBAN VISUALIZATION

The current process of adoption of real-time 3D urban visualization by city planning and urban design departments is similar to the earlier phase of adoption of Geographic Information Systems (GIS) by municipal planning departments. Similar to that experience, a lag of some eight to ten years might be expected between the appearance of the technology in university research centres and implementation in the public sector. There are reasons to believe that there is pressure to move more quickly with real-time urban visualization used with public participation. A prerequisite, however, is that visualization software and 3D virtual city data must be freely and equally accessible to all, rather than having to use custom one-off solutions in terms of data and software. As noted earlier, we are intending to make OrbisRT freely available. This will be our contribution, but budget and staff will be needed to maintain the virtual city models. The pressure to move more quickly to the use of these technologies comes partly from the dramatic reduction in the cost of the hardware for real-time viewing of very complex models. Even more pressure will come from the public becoming used to using Google Earth to view their local urban environment and to be able to build their own models in Sketchup.[21] The only difference between Google Earth and our software is the ability to view far more complex and detailed models in real-time together with more detailed terrain. The program aims to provide the public with urban models accessible over the web that can be viewed at home as well as in public meetings. We feel that the public will demand real-time urban models in the near future. Fortunately, many cities, like the City of Toronto, already have extensive 3D virtual models. They just lack the detail and the ability to be viewed in real-time. Software support for web viewing is already available, though the complexity of models that can be viewed is still limited. There are, for example, already open standards for file formats to allow viewing of 3D models with web browsers such as X3D. There are also standards for combined GIS and 3D modelling data as, for example, CityGML and GeoVRML2. For real-time viewing, gaming engines such as Oblivion and Far Cry are becoming accessible as possible public viewing platforms. They are able to import 3D models in standard file formats. In the future, cities might be able to distribute their models by means of Google Earth. The only real holdback for a massive increase in the use of the technology are the technological hurdles to being able to find more efficient ways

21 Sketchup Model with Google Earth terrain for Yonge-Lawrence neighbourhood, Toronto (2006)

to create visually detailed virtual models in the first place. Photogrammetry and full scale scanning produce models with very detailed geometry, but they are too complex for real-time viewing because that requires simple geometry combined with photographic detail.

CONCLUSIONS

We would like to leave the reader with three conclusions. First, real-time 3D urban visualization coupled with associated abstract information improves urban design outcomes in terms of livable and sustainable cities. Second, technological barriers to the use of this technology have receded; remaining barriers to public involvement are mainly cultural and social. Finally, the cost of not involving the public in developing and visualizing their future city far outweighs the cost of large-scale urban designs 'getting it wrong'. Cities are competing to attract talent to sustain and grow their economies. The costs of getting it wrong can be high.

Landscape Manufacturing
James Kirkpatrick

Gardens have had a strange fate. Their history has almost always anticipated the history of cities. The orchard grid of man's earliest agricultural achievements preceded the layout of the first military cities. The perspectives and diagonals of the Renaissance garden were applied to the squares and colonnades of Renaissance cities. Similarly the romantic, picturesque parks of English empiricism preempted the crescents and arcades of the rich urban design tradition of nineteenth-century English cities. Built exclusively for delight, gardens are like the earliest experiments in that part of architecture that is so difficult to express with words or drawings; pleasure and eroticism. Whether romantic or classical, gardens merge the sensual pleasure of space with the pleasure of reason, in a most useless manner.[1]

Toronto is undergoing a complete urban transformation. For a city whose image has been forever tied to a 550 metre tall tower, the prospect of the city being redefined by what is happening on the ground plane is hard to imagine. More than 700 hectares of public park space is currently being designed and planned across the city. If you were to position that in the heart of Toronto, as Central Park rests in Manhattan, it would be twice the size of the Frederick Law Olmstead masterpiece, and cover an area equivalent to the entire city core.

In almost all cases, these parks are the centerpieces of major new redevelopment districts, being used as infrastructure to seed the creation of new areas of the city. The parks are the first phase of these developments, establishing both the structure and character of the projects. Through open international competitions and requests for proposals, many of the

[1] Tschumi, Bernard, **Architecture and Disjunction**. (New York: The MIT Press, 1996)

Facing Page
2 Competition Entry, Downsview Park Model (OMA/Bruce Mau, 2000)

leading landscape designers are positioned to deliver a new generation of urban parks to the city, previously unseen in Toronto, or any other city at the scale considered. The occupation of Toronto in the coming years has the opportunity to be significantly altered by these new landscapes that not only establish new territories in the city, but also manufacture desire, and potentially create a new identity for the city. In most cases, adjacent development has been anticipated, but the latent potential inherent in the quality of the landscape, and their ability to work cumulatively can reap larger rewards.

As cities look for new boundaries, while trying to mitigate industrial histories, landscape is positioned as the perfect physical and social response to the demands of the evolving urban environment. In relation to other forms of infrastructure, landscape is relatively cheap, quick to construct, and imminently palatable in the development process. Land is becoming scarce in the urban context, and when it is available it is often in the form of brownfield sites available for rehabilitation. Toronto, with fixed borders, and tight budgets, should find creative ways to evolve. Couple these localized realities with large-scale growth strategies like the Places to Grow Act, 'Green Agendas', and the general adoration of all things sustainable, and you have the backdrop for landscape to excel.

The significant park projects planned for Toronto coupled with market forces, world-class designers, and sustainable agendas create an environment to showcase the transformative potential of landscape.

LANDSCAPE MANUFACTURING TERRITORY

The scope of the endeavor in Toronto is unprecedented, but there are lessons to be learned from recent examples that display the power of landscape. As Toronto confronts its potential, New York City, both historically, and in projects currently manifesting themselves, has used open space to great gains. With the Commissioners Plan, New York perfected the grid as urban form, and established the structure of the city; but stepping outside the grid offers many of its most successful open spaces. Central Park was not part of the original grid plan for New York, but soon after, it would swallow up 153 blocks carved out by the grid, not only providing much needed open space at a desperate time in the history of the city, but also creating an address. The diagonal transect of Broadway cuts across the Avenues leaving awkward shaped urban squares within the grid that mark gateways to neighborhoods through their divergence.

And now a new generation of open spaces that work in, around, through, and on top of the grid in Lower Manhattan are recreating a massive portion of the city. With Battery Park City building upon the grid, Hudson River Park working the edges of the grid, Hudson Yards busting through the grid, and the High Line rising above it, open spaces are again being used to breathe new life into the neighborhoods of New York. Infill is inevitable in New York, with constraints and a market unlike anywhere else. But the quality and demand of development can be pushed and pulled, with the driving force in such a dense city as New York having become open space.

If Central Park and Broadway represented old money, then the generation of parks led by the High Line represents new money.

Central Park was the ultimate piece of open space infrastructure. Not only did it take on a host of necessary functions in a growing Manhattan, it spurred the development and occupation of much of the city. Its influences are still being felt today, and with the recent sale of a condominium on Central Park West fetching $50 million, the largest sum ever paid for an apartment in North America, and presumably the world, its value has not diminished.

Central Park pushed the boundaries of Manhattan, and in so doing created a niche for the role of the urban park. At a time when public open space was not a priority, Central Park showed the potential of urban parks. Not long after, Olmstead was filling out sites in Brooklyn, Boston, and Montreal with his grand, green visions that were followed shortly by new neighborhoods. Olmstead laid the foundation for the profession of landscape architecture with Central Park, along with it he established a role for public open space in the city; a role in developing new frontiers for growth, in creating new locations, and beneath it all, in creating desire.

LANDSCAPE MANUFACTURING DESIRE

This connection between open space and desire is now being played out in its most concentrated form of spectacle in New York, where public open space has fully engaged its capitalist environs and become commodity. An elevated rail line that cuts through the west side of Manhattan transformed into a beguiling open space, the High Line, and is creating a new address in the city.

> Someday, around a year from now, one of your friends is going to say to you, 'Let's go to the High Line.' Now, this person might be talking about the High Line park, the well-publicized ribbon of greenery that's being constructed on an abandoned elevated rail line in far west Chelsea, running north from Gansevoort all the way to 34th Street. Or your friend might be referring to the High Line neighborhood: the new skyline of glittering retail spaces and restaurants and condos, designed by brand-name architects like Frank Gehry and Jean Nouvel and Robert A.M. Stern, with names like the High Line Building and High Line 519 and HL23. Or your friend might mean the High Line Terrace and Lounge in the new condo tower at 245 Tenth, which promises prospective residents views over the High Line, along with "polished cervaiole marble floors." Or maybe your friend wants to go to the Highline Thai restaurant on Washington Street, or the High Line Ballroom, a recently opened concert venue, which, starting May 9, will be part of the High Line Festival, an event curated by David Bowie and showcasing such snazzy right-now artists as Ricky Gervais and Arcade Fire.[3]

From its celebrity board members to its neighboring developments designed by celebrity architects, the High Line has itself become celebrity,

3 Adam Sternbergh, 'The High Line: It Brings Good Things to Life,' **New York Magazine**: (www.nymag.com/news/features/31273/)

[4] Image here is used in reference to Guy Debord's **Society of the Spectacle**, where he described images as the agents of the spectacle, 'In societies where modern conditions of production prevail, all of life presents itself as an immense accumulation of spectacles. Everything that was directly lived has moved away into a representation.' Guy Debord, **Society of the Spectacle**. (Detroit: Black & Red, 1987).

[5] Editorial, 'High Line should be part of Hudson Yards,' **The Villager** (http://www.thevillager.com/villager_240/editorial.html).

and in the process transformed from what was once a grassroots community heritage preservation project into an image[4]. The words High Line now resonate with the same cache as the Comme des Garçons store that lies in its shadow.

Before construction even began on the High Line Park, a two point six kilometer long elevated park, development projects started to pop up all around, anticipating the open space. Now that construction is well under way, the glut of projects has not relented, and the value added by the adjacency of the High Line is 20 percent or more[5] compared to other properties in the neighborhood without proximity to the park.

The High Line has taken on an extreme identity, more so than any other park space in the city, even Central Park, because it has become so quantifiable as an image, as a commodity that people desire. The High Line has celebrity endorsers like Edward Norton and Kevin Bacon who sit on its Board, its own festival curated by David Bowie, T-shirts that they hand out at public hearings, multiple books, all before it has even opened to the public. The marketing of the park has created something so distant from the original intention of the park—a heritage preservation project—but the object that has been created can prove more valuable than the park itself.

The greatest function that the High Line is performing is not its own manifestation but the rampant desire it has created for open spaces, in concentrating desire for parks. While opponents complain that the rich are getting richer in terms of the location and clientele that the park is serving with its increasingly rich neighbors, the High Line is raising the value of the idea of parks everywhere in the city, and beyond. The ancillary value created by the park, and the demand it has created will allow other projects to happen that may not have otherwise. Its resiliency fought off the effects of 9/11, which soured development in south Manhattan, and it has fueled other competitions and visionary open spaces in New York, such as Fresh Kills Park, and Gateway National Park. Much like Central Park foretold a generation of large urban parks, the High Line can trigger not only local redevelopment, but also an international fervor for glamorous new open spaces.

LANDSCAPE MANUFACTURING IDENTITY

While Toronto and its planned parks might not have the cache of New York or the High Line just yet, the city has managed to attract the focus of the entire profession of landscape architecture. Downsview Park started the process with a design competition roughly ten years ago that brought Toronto to the attention of some of the brightest design thinkers in the world. While the ensuing implementation hasn't managed to sustain the enthusiasm, a slew of other projects and competitions in its wake have secured Downsview's importance in repositioning Toronto in the international design scene. Downsview has left a legacy, both from a design standpoint, as a harbinger of many of the landscape urbanism concepts that dominate contemporary park design, and as a process, from the many competitions that have followed in Toronto and abroad. It brought landscape to the pages of architecture magazines again, and created a public dialogue on new forms of open space, only to seemingly disappear.

With Downsview again showing signs of life, and a rapid succession of competitions churning out new park designs on the waterfront, momentum in Toronto is starting to build again. The new projects join Downsview as parks mostly planned in liminal areas traditionally associated with industrial histories. Parts of the city that have long been disregarded will be transformed by parks that will create entirely new urban boundaries and zones of intensity for Toronto. What these projects lack that High Line has, is the inspirational quality of a singular vision.

Downsview Park, Lower Don Lands Park, Lake Ontario Park, Commissioner's Park, Don Valley Brickworks, Nathan Philips Square, The Central Waterfront, HtO, CityPlace Park, and Sherbourne Park highlight a massive amount of marquee open space planned in the city. Many of the proposed parks are on the waterfront, as part of Waterfront Toronto's Public Space Framework, but there is an opportunity to understand the benefits of all of these parks working as a system. From events being planned in conflict, such as public open houses for Donlands Park and Nathan Philips Square on the same night, to Parks 'canceling each other out' as with the recent Lower Don Park competition enveloping previous efforts by the same agency for Commissioner's Park, clearly there is a disconnect for a larger vision. Whereas the High Line has gone from pipe dream to construction in eight years, Toronto struggles to build consensus. The lack of overall vision or marketing, combined with a lack of actual built progress, has created great skepticism among the public, especially in regards to the waterfront work.

Tangential to these parks projects, the city has also begun developing a Parks Renaissance strategy:

> The Parks Renaissance Strategy is a reinvestment program that will align the City's parks, trails and physical assets with the social, economic and cultural needs of residents. The Strategy will serve as a framework for decision-making and investment. It will include a set of guiding principles for improving parks, trails and facilities to achieve targets and goals, and respond to diverse and changing populations.[6]

6 www.toronto.ca/parks/renaissance.htm

While documents like this are useful strategic tools for municipalities, the celebrity potential of the major parks provides the fuel to start rebuilding the image of the cities parks. If these projects can be presented in unison as part of a system, then their transformative potential can extend beyond their local and participate at a citywide scale and capture civic interest. The renaissance happening with Toronto's cultural institutions, at the hands of internationally renown architects in the form of The Royal Ontario Museum by Daniel Libeskind, The Art Gallery of Ontario by Frank Gehry, the Ontario College of Art & Design by Will Alsop, and work by some of Canada's leading practitioners at The Four Seasons Centre, Gardiner Ceramic Museum, Canada's National Ballet School, and Royal Conservatory School of Music, pales in comparison to the latent city-building potential in the landscapes being proposed.

But because the parks don't share the iconic nature of buildings, the importance of what is happening on the ground in Toronto has gone largely unnoticed. Toronto has been begging for years for an Olympic event, World's Fair, or some other significant event to transform itself. While the event would bring international attention, the city is most interested in reaping the long-term infrastructure improvements from the event. It is possible to view the park renaissance as the catalyst for the transformation. But because it isn't happening under the uniform banner of a singular event, the full scope of this undertaking hasn't dawned on a city that is constantly in search of a means of defining itself. Toronto doesn't have the picturesque backdrop of Vancouver, or the romantic charm of Montreal, and it has for years hung its hat on the concrete spire of the CN tower; now it has a chance to establish a lasting and evolving identity for itself in the form of one of the best and most eclectic open space systems in the world.

LANDSCAPES MANUFACTURING FUTURES

We live in a world where image is all-important. As was foreseen by Debord and McLuhan, everything we experience and understand is mediated to us through images. But parks by their nature belie image. The natural, growing, ever-evolving system of a park isn't easily reducible to a singular image, thus providing a potential escape from the trappings of our capitalist construct. Not only a respite from the noise and furor of the city, the park is also a chance to escape image. But now as images become ever dominant, as the line blurs between politicians and celebrities, as scandals overtake wars in the headlines, the High Line has shown that even open space can be reduced to commodity. But this image can be used to fuel development, and spur urban redevelopment. As the parks continue to grow they will provide a constantly shifting image to the city, outlasting the ephemeral nature of traditional images—and at the scale of the undertaking in Toronto, the parks can transcend image and become identity.

Each new open space is a seed, sowing a new neighborhood in the city. In recent history Toronto has used small urban interventions, like Yorkville Park, and Dundas Square to reinvigorate densely urban parts of the city. Now it looks for parks to rebuild parts of the city at a much larger scale, mostly along its neglected waterfront but also through new outposts such as Downsview Park. Toronto has seen little in the way of new open space for years, but now a major new generation is about to unfold.

The important first step has been taken, by securing the best talent in the world, through open international competitions and proposal calls. Now these parks must come to life, to start to sow the same results that other cities have achieved, but on a much larger scale as part of a unified vision.

The view from the top of the CN Tower doesn't provide a view of the concrete city that many perceive Toronto to be, but rather it lays out a green carpet, an unending canopy of trees that dominates the city. Toronto sits at the threshold of an opportunity to extend and enhance that 'green' and shift its identity from the vertical peak of its famous tower to the horizontal expanse of its park land.

Ravine City and Farm City
Chris Hardwicke

IMPORTANCE OF CITIES

Over the course of the twentieth century, humanity was involved in an unprecedented experiment: we have become a predominantly urban species. The majority of us now live in large cities. In one century our urban populations have grown from 15 percent to 50 percent of the total population. Cities have always been dependent on their peripheries. As urban sprawl grows to consume valuable agricultural land, agricultural lands are increasingly encroaching on sensitive wilderness areas. Cities are putting pressures on ecosystems and are using the biosphere, the water system and the atmosphere as storage for their ecological debt.

This paper proposes rethinking the city-nature relationship by integrating urban systems with natural ecosystems in two visionary projects for the city of Toronto: Ravine City and Farm City. 'Ravine City' is a proposed urban ecosystem of collective housing that restores and enhances the ravine system of Toronto. 'Farm City' is a project that creates agricultural area inside new housing towers, and produces living and growing space in a dense vertical format. Both models attempt to renew our connection to our natural resources.

CITY ECOFOOTPRINTS

Cities have two footprints on the land: their actual urban footprint, and an ecological footprint, which extends far beyond the urban, suburban, and agricultural areas surrounding the city. Take Toronto as an example of the effects of urban sprawl: like most large modern cities, it has an enormous environmental impact. The estimated ecological footprint of Toronto impacts an area over 280 times its size. By the year 2015, the area is expected to increase 55 percent even without an increase in population.[1] Of that ecological footprint only 20 percent is created by housing. The majority of the footprint comes from food (31 percent) and transportation (24 percent).

[1] M. Wackernagel et al. How Big is Toronto's Ecological Footprint? (Centre for Sustainability Studies and the City of Toronto, 1998)

Facing Page
[2] View of rooftop gardens overlooking ravine, Ravine City

Even contemporary environmental approaches assume human habitation's negative effect on the world. Terms like 'self-sufficient', 'sustainable', 'carbon neutral', and 'off the grid' are used to describe our current environmental aspirations for buildings. These terms reflect limited goals that assume that little or no impact is the best we can do.

But natural systems do not operate at the scale of a building. They extend as a network to the scale of the city, region, and biosphere. Healthy cities must integrate their urban systems with natural systems at the same scale. Green buildings alone will not produce a significant change in our effect on the environment. Instead of going 'off the grid' we should be connecting to and supplying the grid by creating cyclical networks that create more than they consume.

There are no ecosystems untouched by human activity, and there are worrying signs that the world's ecosystems are reaching the limits of their ability to adapt to human impacts.

Ravine City and Farm City look at how an existing modern city like Toronto can evolve over time towards productive systems using urban ecosystem planning. These projects look at how to integrate food, water, transportation, and housing over time in an existing city.

ECOSYSTEM DESIGN

Toronto, like most modern cities, is based on linear dependent systems to support its needs. Resources are funneled through a linear dependent system without concern about their origin and destination of wastes. Our urban sewage systems, for example, separate people from their wastes. Sewage is usually discharged downstream and its inherent fertility is lost to farmland.

This linear metabolic system is unnatural and unsustainable. Natural systems are cyclical: every output from a natural organism is also an input, which renews and sustains the larger living environment. As our world becomes predominantly urban we need to adopt an ecosystem approach to designing and planning our cities.

The word 'ecosystem' derives its meaning from the Greek word 'oikos' meaning 'house, dwelling place, habitation'. Ravine City and Farm City connect the original meaning of oikos with ecosystems to propose housing that gives back to the system by participating in the flows of the larger network. In these projects urban outputs are seen as crucial inputs into urban systems producing, recycling, and generating productive wastes into energy and food.

RAVINE CITY

Ravine City is a visionary proposal for an urban system of collective housing that restores and enhances the ravine system of Toronto. The project uses the continuous watershed and ecosystem of the ravines as a model for urban infrastructure and renews our connection to nature.

RAVINES AND CULTURE

The Toronto Ravine System is the defining natural feature of the city. Interrupting the street grid with wide green valleys, the ravines house the most diverse ecosystems in the urban area. Toronto ravines have inspired works of art and literature as well as being a central natural resource for the City. The ravines appear prominently in the works of writers such as Morley Callaghan, Margaret Atwood, Anne Michaels, Michael Ondaatje, and Ann-Marie MacDonald. Robert Fulford has written that the ravines 'are the shared subconscious of the municipality, the places where much of the city's literature is born.'[3]

3 Robert Fulford, 'Toronto & Margaret Atwood.' The National Post (August 24, 2000)

HISTORY OF THE RAVINES

Toronto's ravines were formed twelve thousand years ago after the end of the ice age. Rivers and creeks cut deep ravines through the Toronto region. The largest ravines run south from the Oak Ridges Moraine to Lake Ontario.

The history of the Toronto ravines traces our collective relationship with nature. Originally the ravines were a source of fuel, food, water, and pleasure. Since the 1800s we have polluted, channeled, buried, dumped, logged, and sewered most of our ravines.

Early settlers extensively logged the ravines and used the rivers as a source of power for water mills. Clay from the ravines was the source of most of the bricks that built the Victorian city. Early photographs of the ravines show that they were always a source of pleasure and recreation. Settlers used the ravines for swimming and bathing, fishing, hiking, gathering, boating, and skating.

Although the ravines were an essential natural resource for early Torontonians they were seen as an interruption of the street grid and as a breeding ground for pests and disease. The largest river, the Don River, was engineered in a concrete channel to minimize flooding and protect industrial lands. Many of the ravines have almost completely disappeared under the city. Both Garrison Creek and Taddle Creek, which ran through the downtown, were sewered and almost completely buried. Garrison Creek was originally as wide as ninety-one meters and up to twenty-one meters deep.

Only the largest ravines remain today: the Humber River, the Don River, and the Rouge River. For the most part Toronto has turned its back on most of the surviving ravines. The Don Valley was significantly cut off from the city by rail lines and later an expressway. We have bridged, fenced, and bypassed the ravines to the point that many people are entirely unaware of the ravines around them. The engineering of our ravines was a modern project that reflected the western attitude toward nature as a wild force to be subdued and civilized.

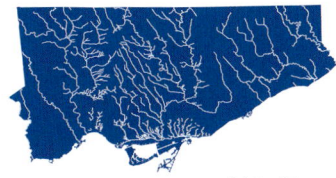

Original Rivers

Current Rivers

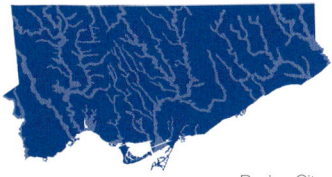

Ravine City

4 Toronto rivers over time, Ravine City

REVIVAL OF THE RAVINES

Only recently has Toronto begun to re-appreciate its ravines as a significant natural and recreational resource. The ravines have remained in our subconscious as a kind of repressed nature. Groups like Friends of the Don, Toronto Region Conservation Authority, and projects like the Human River, and Lost Rivers are interested in the protection and restoration of the ravines. In 2002, the City of Toronto issued the Ravine Protection By-law protecting ravine lands.

The ravines are now extensively used for recreational activities as part of a pattern of trails, parks, and open spaces that are loosely connected to the hidden ravine system. The ravines today are popular with runners, roller bladers, hikers, and cyclists but the rivers are still quite polluted, preventing swimming, and wading. Despite these activities most of the ravines remain disconnected from the city.

WATER SYSTEMS AND CITIES

Water supports all life on our planet. The world's water supply is finite and our water use is growing exponentially. While the world's population tripled in the twentieth century, the use of water resources has grown six-fold. As our population grows there will be an increased demand for water, which will have serious consequences on the environment.

In a natural hydrological cycle water moves through the environment by the processes of precipitation, run-off, infiltration, evaporation, and condensation. Most rainfall infiltrates the ground. In cities like Toronto most of the natural infiltration is prevented by impervious surfaces such as rooftops, roads, and parking lots. Rainwater is collected and channeled into the storm water sewer system: a vast hidden infrastructure. As rainwater flows across hard surfaces it picks up pollutants such as heavy metals, oil, grease, chemicals, animal waste, pesticides, bacteria, and phosphorus and is discharged into rivers, streams, and ultimately, Lake Ontario.

In the older areas of Toronto, combined sewers, which carry sanitary sewage and storm water in the same pipe, continue to divert excess flow into our natural watercourses. In times of high rainfall excess flow is diverted from water pollution treatment plants into the nearest watercourse. Very large storms produce flows that rush into our streams and rivers, eroding stream banks, and causing flooding. As Toronto's urban development continues to place stress on our watercourses, flooding and pollution will continue to be a significant risk. Although we have agencies, like the Toronto Region Conservation Authority that manage and protect our watersheds, they operate in isolated silos. Housing, transportation, parks, and public works operate as independent agencies disconnected from our natural systems. Our political, zoning, and decision-making processes rely on arbitrary boundaries that follow the street grid or river centerlines rather than bioregions or watershed boundaries.

Events like the Walkerton enquiry[5] remind us that we can no longer make isolated decisions. We continue to allow contaminated storm water and the degradation of our rivers to threaten the health of our waters. Ravine City proposes using the watershed boundaries as political and planning boundaries, ensuring a direct relationship with the larger ecosystem.

HOUSING IN RAVINE CITY

Each home in Ravine City is an integral part of the ravine system. The housing development forms an artificial ravine that runs along the top edge of the existing Toronto ravines. The housing's terraced roofs are connected together to create an artificial ravine. This encourages a continuous connected ecosystem. The artificial ravine functions much like the natural ravines: controlling water flow and regeneration as well as cleaning the air, creating habitat, and biomass. Maintained and operated by the City, this new topographic infrastructure is connected to the natural ravine system and operates as a second level of public open space.

---

5 In May 2000, seven residents of Walkerton, Ontario, died, and hundreds more became seriously ill as a result of the contamination of the town's water supply.

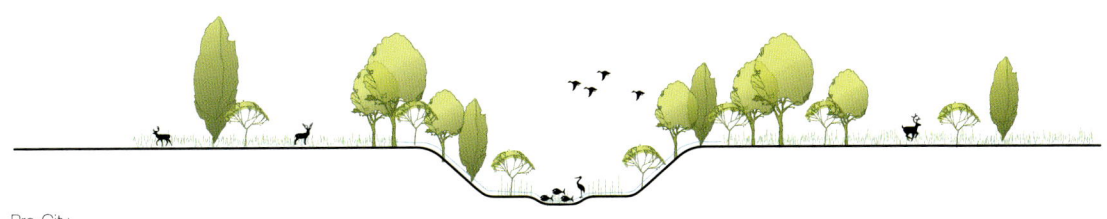
Pre-City

Victorian City

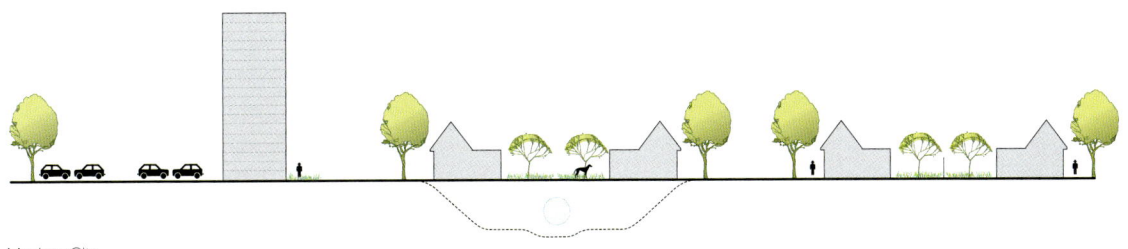
Modern City

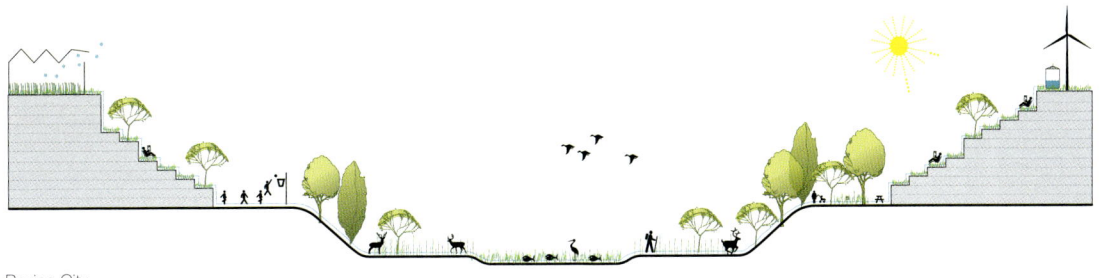
Ravine City

6 Ravine sections over time, Ravine City

Ravine City and Farm City | 100

Ravine City proposes to reduce the need for costly storm water sewers and drainage by restoring the buried ravine system of Toronto and developing dense housing, which functions as a network of green roofs that connect to the natural water systems of our ravines.

NETWORKS IN RAVINE CITY

Conventional roofing systems are the most expensive parts of a building to maintain. They are exposed to the sun, dramatic variations in temperature, and next to roads, they are the largest impervious surface in our urban environment. By activating the roof system of Ravine City and connecting it to the public space and ecological network, the new surface becomes a productive part of the urban fabric.

In ecosystems, the role of diversity is closely connected with the system's network structure. A diverse ecosystem is resilient because it contains many species with overlapping ecological functions that can partially replace one another. The housing in Ravine City follows this model. Rather than have each housing unit act as a self-sufficient entity, every unit in Ravine City, in addition to its housing functions, acts as an individual species with a particular function. Each building contributes as a generator and distributor within the urban ecosystem. Some houses are predominantly solar generators. Others are wind generators, urban farms, wastewater treatments, storm water retainers, urban forests, or recreational areas, and so on. These units generate a surplus of nutrients, energy, or restoration and share their surplus with the community. Each unit is interconnected to create a flexible and resilient urban network.

The flexibility of the system is fundamental to the sustainability of Ravine City. As changes in technology, population, climate, and culture happen over time, the distribution of different ecological housing types can be incrementally changed to adapt. Each type follows simple specifications that, when combined with the others, create a robust system that can respond to local and regional fluctuations.

RESTORE THE RAVINES

Over time, the original Toronto ravine system would be restored and enhanced as part of the Ravine City project. The connected artificial and natural ravine systems would create an open space system that would act as a shared cultural and environmental resource. In Ravine City, housing would sustain the whole community and the extended territory allowing everyone to contribute to the health of the city and region. Ravine City makes natural cycle visible and brings the ravines into Toronto's daily consciousness. Most importantly, Ravine City reconnects the city to the pleasure of its greatest natural resource.

FARM CITY

Farm City proposes a new kind of architecture that would enable cities to feed themselves by creating agricultural areas inside new housing towers. By combining living and growing spaces in a dense vertical format, Farm City reduces the need for sprawling suburbs, eliminates food travel distance, and creates a living architecture that is part of an urban ecosystem. Farm City allows urban

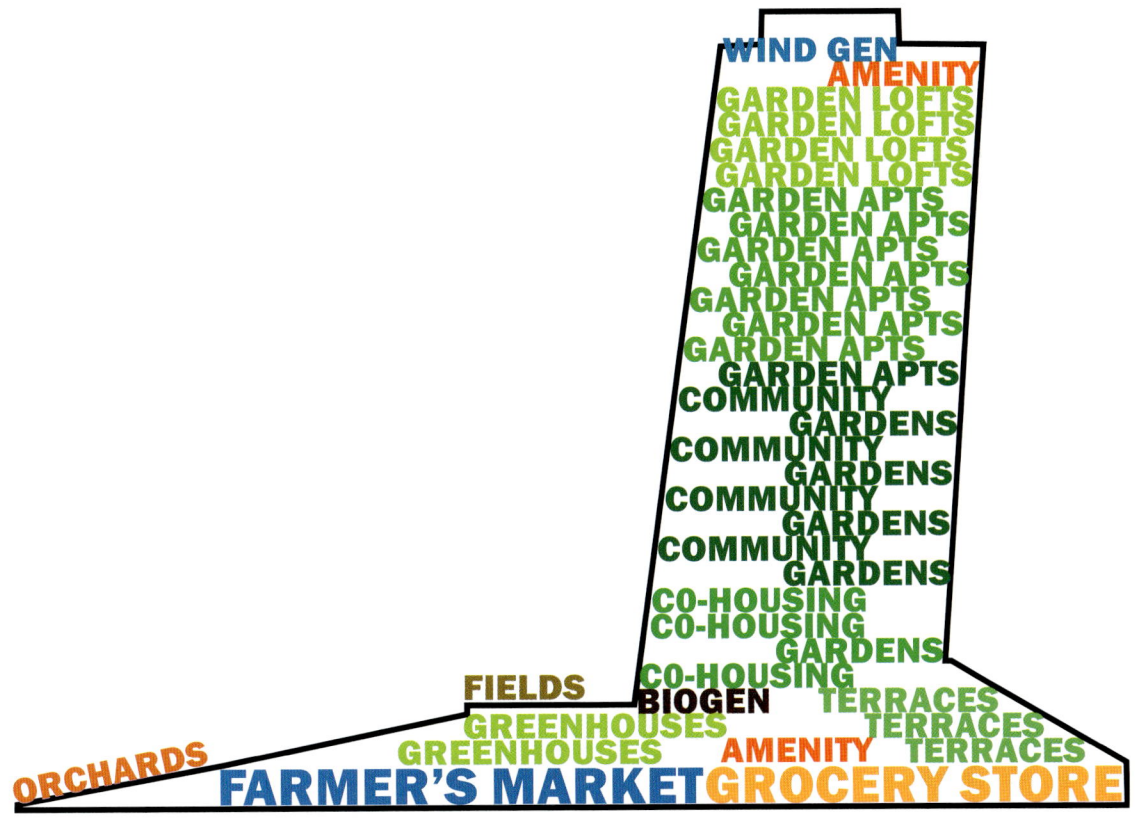

7 Program Section, Farm City

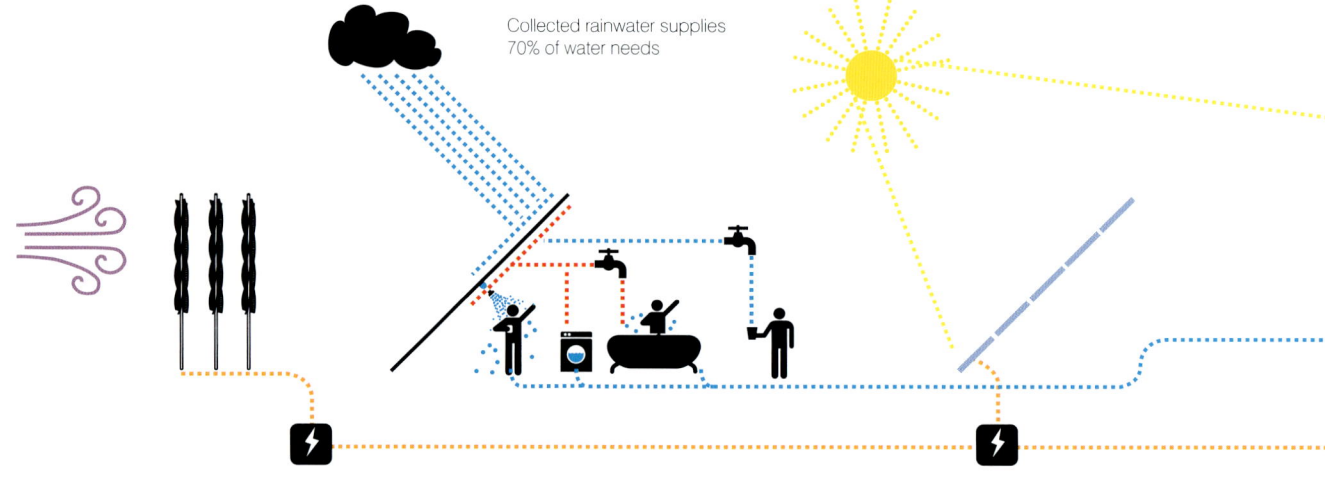

Wind turbines on the roof generate 60% of the electricity needs

Waste heat from greenhouses supplies 90% of heating

Solar panels supply 20% of the electricity needs

dwellers to be responsible for the production of their food: to be farmers or gardeners. Farm City is a place where we can watch our food grow and take delight in our own sustenance.

AGRICULTURE AND SPACE

Worldwide, over 38 percent of the total landmass of the earth (800 million hectares) is used for agriculture. In the next fifty years, the world population is expected to rise to at least 8.6 billion, which would require an additional 10 billion hectares of agricultural land. That quantity of farmland is not presently available.

The Greater Toronto Area (GTA) is the fastest growing city in Canada, adding a 100,000 new people a year. Between 1976 and 1996, the GTA lost 62,000 hectares of farmland to development, with another 40,000 hectares designated for development. It is projected that by the year 2026, 40 percent of all agricultural land in the GTA will have been lost to development.[8]

FOOD SYSTEM

A food system is the chain of activities connecting food production, processing, distribution, consumption, and waste management. Not only does it include the diverse agricultural system, it also includes the natural resource base, such as soil fertility and water systems.

Food systems have always had spatial consequences. Despite this, the land use implications of food systems are not being addressed in Toronto. There is a neglect of agriculture in urban planning policy. Current discussions about food

8 Sean Cosgrove. 'Food Secure City: Toronto Food Policy Council Submission to the Toronto Official Plan' (Toronto Food Policy Counci, 2000), 8

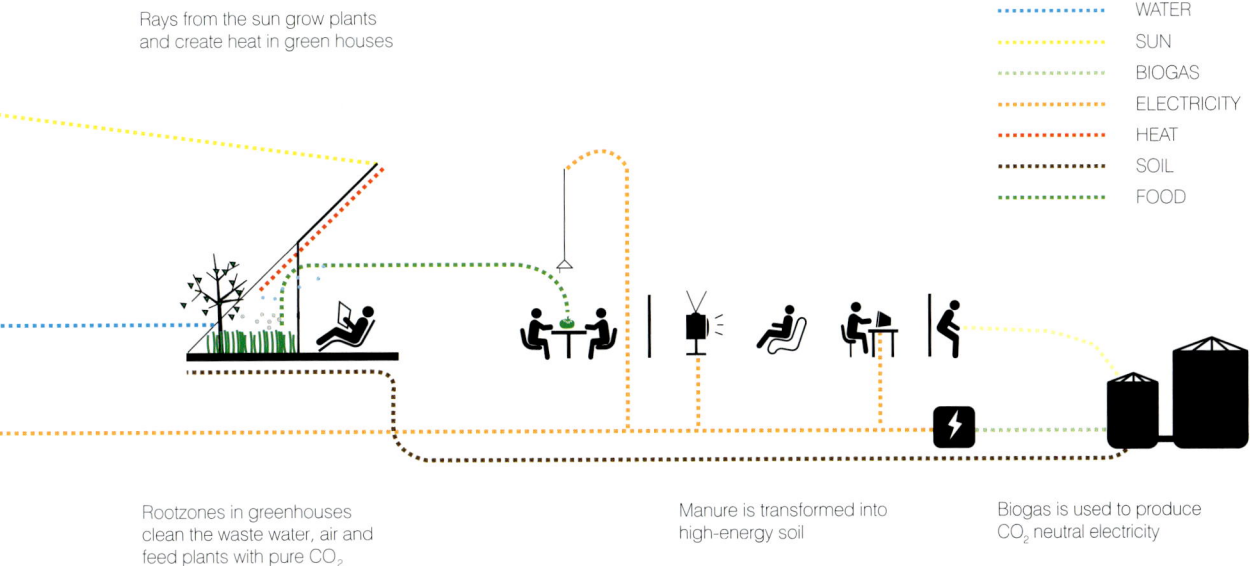

9 Energy Cycle, Farm City

systems largely ignore the spatial consequences. Currently, in the City of Toronto, there is no zoning for agricultural uses. Land values within cities relegate garden spaces to marginal sites and city dwellers are increasingly trying to persuade the city to give them space for growing crops. As our population grows, our food production will have a greater impact on land use and the landscape.

CONTEMPORARY FARMING AND HEALTH

Contemporary farming has transformed our landscapes from wilderness to fields for crops and herds, and has devastated ecosystems through erosion, pollution, and clearing. Although contemporary agricultural practices undeniably contribute to our good health and longevity, it is becoming more and more apparent that they are creating new health hazards at an unprecedented scale. Traditional agricultural practices that use significant amounts of agrochemicals such as pesticides and fungicides present significant risks. Agricultural and urban encroachments into natural areas have increased the occurrence of emerging infections such as respiratory diseases, influenza, rabies, yellow fever, and malaria.

FARM CITY AND PROXIMITY

Farm City proposes we bring food production back into the city. The proximity of the food production would allow us to oversee our agricultural practices and ensure that they are safe. Keeping food production within our cities would stop the further encroachment of agricultural lands into our wilderness, and allow our forests and wetlands to regenerate. These ecosystems are not only great natural

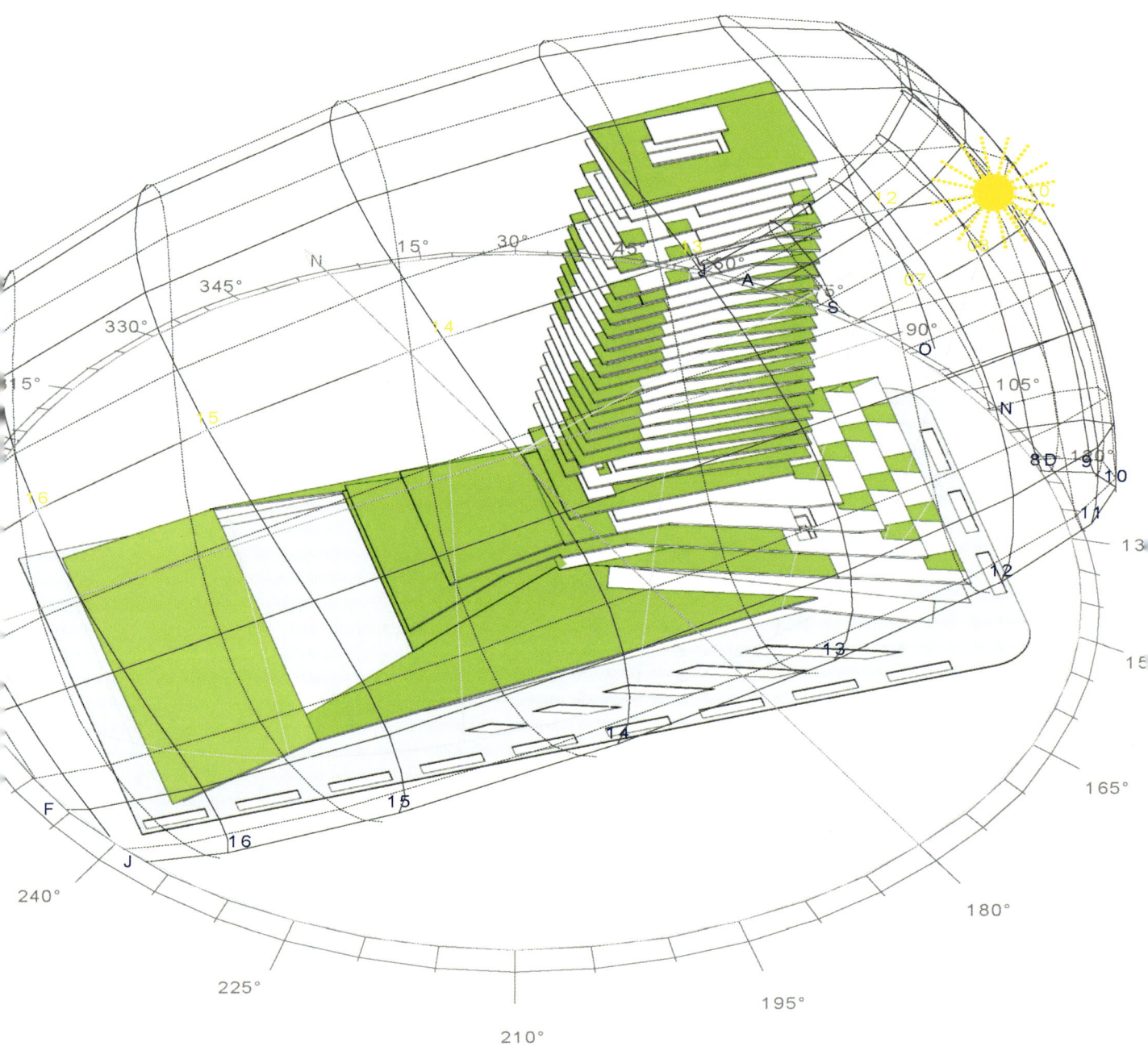

10 Growing Areas and Solar Orientation, Farm City

resources, but are essential to creating cleaner air and safer drinking water, as well as reversing climate change.

INDOOR FARMING

Indoor farming is not a new idea. Tomatoes, strawberries and a wide variety of herbs have been grown in greenhouses for years. Urban farming is not a new idea either. People have always grown food in backyards, community gardens, and vacant land within cities. Farm City is the vertical extension of urban agriculture using greenhouse technologies. It creates more area for growing and allows apartment dwellers access to gardens.

HOUSING AND INDOOR FARMING

By locating housing and farms in the same building, Farm City creates symbiotic relationships between energy, water, and waste. Heat generated from the greenhouses is used to heat the housing units. Biomass from the greenhouses is used for energy. Solar energy is generated from the large glazed surface. Grey-water and compost generated from the housing is used in the greenhouses.

FARM CITY BENEFITS

Farm City contributes to the health of our city socially, economically, and environmentally. Urban agriculture can have different purposes: subsistence and food security, city ecology improvement, and income and employment generation. Farm City helps conserve soils and minimize waste. It also improves microclimate, nutrient recycling, water management, biodiversity, and CO_2 balance. Most importantly, it makes food production part of our culture by making gardens visible and allowing us to participate in our own sustenance.

URBAN IMAGE

Cities have become the stage where the future of our civilization and the biosphere will be determined. Our planet will not be able to accommodate growing cities that continue to draw upon distant resources. Ravine City and Farm City challenge the traditional urban image of the city as a collection of individual buildings and properties. Architecture becomes a part of the landscape. Housing is connected to a living social network that follows the flow of natural systems.

ACTION

DOUGLAS MACLEOD Towards a Design Nation
LARISSA MULLER
DAVID COVO
RICHARD LEVY

Towards a Design Nation
Douglas MacLeod, Larissa Muller, David Covo and Richard Levy[1]

> In a global economy, design is becoming a critical competitive advantage [2]
> Roger Martin

[1] This paper is based on a study prepared by the authors for the Asia Pacific Foundation of Canada entitled Design as an Instrument of Public Policy in Singapore and South Korea

[2] Roger Martin is the Dean of the Rotman School of Management at the University of Toronto. Quote published in B. Breen, 'The Business of Design,' **Fast Company** (April 2005), 69.

[3] Designed by Canadian-born Karim Rashid for Toronto-based Umbra, the Garbo garbage can has sold 7 million copies world wide

[4] K. W. Chung, 'Strategies for Promoting Korean Design Excellence,' **Design Issues** (Vol. 14, No. 2, 1998), 4

A successful economy ultimately depends on the sale of goods and services, and it is worth emphasizing that consumers make purchases based not on the science or research invested in a good, but largely because they want them. Creating that perception is not based on technology, infrastructure, or legislation (although all these things can make a contribution) but on design. Put another way, the most innovative manufacturing processes and distribution networks in the world are pointless unless people want the goods they produce. iPods, Blackberries, PT Cruisers, VW Beetles, and Garbo garbage cans[3] all demonstrate the tremendous economic power of good design. According to one study carried out in the late 1990s, Koreans ranked brand image (44.7 percent) and design (29.1 percent) as the two most important factors influencing their purchases of consumer electronics.[4]

There is also a direct correlation between good design and success factors such as productivity, innovation, and global competitiveness. When supported by good design, new technologies, infrastructure, and even legislation can level the playing field for small and medium sized enterprises and provide significant advantages for those nations that deploy them first. In this context, design can create value for Canada in terms of its global competitiveness, its ongoing sustainability, its productivity, and its capacity for innovation.

VALUE OF DESIGN

According to the World Economic Forum, Canada's ranking in their Global Competitiveness Report has slipped from thirteenth in 2005 to sixteenth in 2006 which reflects an ongoing trend—Canada was fifth in the world in 1999.[11] This trend must be considered in light of Canada's unique economic situation: it exports 45 percent of its manufacturing output—more than any other industrialized nation. In 2005 this amounted to $436.2 billion CAD[5]. According to previous studies conducted by the Asia Pacific Foundation of Canada, purchasing decisions are often influenced by where a product was made. If branding Canada as a 'design nation' resulted in only a 1 percent increase in exports it would increase our trade surplus by over $4 billion.

As further evidence of the economic value of design, the U.K. Design Council has tracked the progress of sixty-three firms that used 'high-quality' design since 1994 in what they have called the U.K. Design Index. Over the last thirteen years these companies have outperformed the London Stock Exchange's FTSE Index by 200 percent in good times and bad.[6]

In terms of sustainability, Natural Resources Canada has determined that some 30 percent of the greenhouse gases emitted in Canada come from the heating and cooling of buildings. Other sources suggest that when the additional greenhouse gases embedded in the manufacture of building materials is factored into this, figures rise as high as 48 percent.[7] Vancouver-based architect Peter Busby estimates that the building industry alone could reduce its greenhouse gas emissions by 50 percent at minimal cost. As the issue of global warming grows in importance, Canadian expertise in this area may become a valuable export.

Some simple design measures such as improved daylighting have been shown to increase productivity and reduce absenteeism by significant amounts at companies such as Lockheed and Boeing. One building with enhanced daylighting at Lockheed Martin's sprawling office complex in Sunnyvale, California has been said to have saved them $500,000 US each year in reduced energy costs and decreased absenteeism by as much as 15 percent.

Other measures, based on new technologies, can also improve the productivity of the design, manufacturing, and construction industries. Rapid prototyping equipment can help speed the flow of designs from 'file to factory' and collaborative communications tools can allow teams in different countries to co-design and peer produce products and assemblies. Co-design and peer production refer to the idea of distributing these activities across a distributed network of specialists who combine their expertise to create, develop, and refine products more quickly and efficiently. Most importantly, all of these tools and capabilities can be shared across broadband networks to make them accessible to small and medium sized enterprises (SMEs) as well as large corporations.

There is also a clear correlation between high quality design and innovation. One Finnish study noted that '... perhaps it is not worth even trying to separate innovation and design, because they strongly influence each other'.[8] Finland, with a population of only five million people, ranks fourth in the world in terms of innovation and second in the world in terms of overall global competitiveness. (Canada's rankings are thirteen and sixteen respectively).[9]

Finally, although it is more difficult to quantify, design also impacts our quality of life. Healthier, more stimulating, and more accessible environments; products that are a delight to use; and services that are both functional and engaging, are all the result of good design.

[5] www.strategis.ic.gc.ca/sc_mrkti/tdst/tdo/tdo.php#tag, 1/15/07

[6] www.designcouncil.org.uk

[7] www.architecture2030.org/building_sector/index.html, 1/15/07

[8] M. Linström and M. Nyberg, 'ETLA,' **Designfacts** (Volume 1), 2-4. Available online at www.tekes.fi/ohjelmat/muoto.

[9] Ibid

GLOBAL DESIGN

[10] Patrick Whitney, principal of the IIT Institute of Design, **China Daily** (June 12, 2005), 11

The centre of gravity, energy and growth of the design market is shifting from North America to Asia.[10]

Patrick Whitney

The table to the right ranks the components of the design strategies of various nations.[12] The section below outlines how other countries from around the world are investing in design. The common elements of such strategies include:

- i   National Design Policies
- ii   Design Infrastructure: Centres and Networks
- iii   Engaging SMEs
- iv   Design Education & Training
- v   Branding, Marketing and Dissemination
- vi   Design Knowledge Management
- vii   The Role of Governments
- viii   The Role of the Private Sector

Many countries, particularly in the Asia Pacific region, have, or are building, national design strategies:

India has prepared a National Design Strategy that was approved early in 2007. It will address education, use of design by SMEs, intellectual property, branding, and design exports.

Singapore has developed and is implementing the Design Singapore Initiative as its first national collaborative strategy, which includes facilitating the use of design by business, establishing design testbeds, and establishing a national design council.

In 2003, the government of New Zealand announced it would invest over $10 million CAD in a five year strategy to disseminate information about design, assist businesses to make better use of design, and improve the quality of design education.

In 2002 the government of Taiwan announced a Cultural and Creative Industries Development Plan as part of its Challenge 2008: Taiwan Development Plan with a goal of using innovation, design, and branding as a means of upgrading and enhancing Taiwanese business.

The Republic of Korea, however, has one of the most comprehensive national design strategies of any nation. In the 1990s when Korean goods became less competitive due to price, the government's Committee for Globalization Policy began the development of a national design agenda. During the last fifteen years Korea has implemented three five-year plans in design—from 1993-1997, from 1998-2002 and the recent plan which began in 2003 and was completed in 2007. The aim of these plans was that by 2007 the country's design industries would be on a par with those of developed countries with dramatically increased employment opportunities for designers and a general increase in design awareness by the general public.

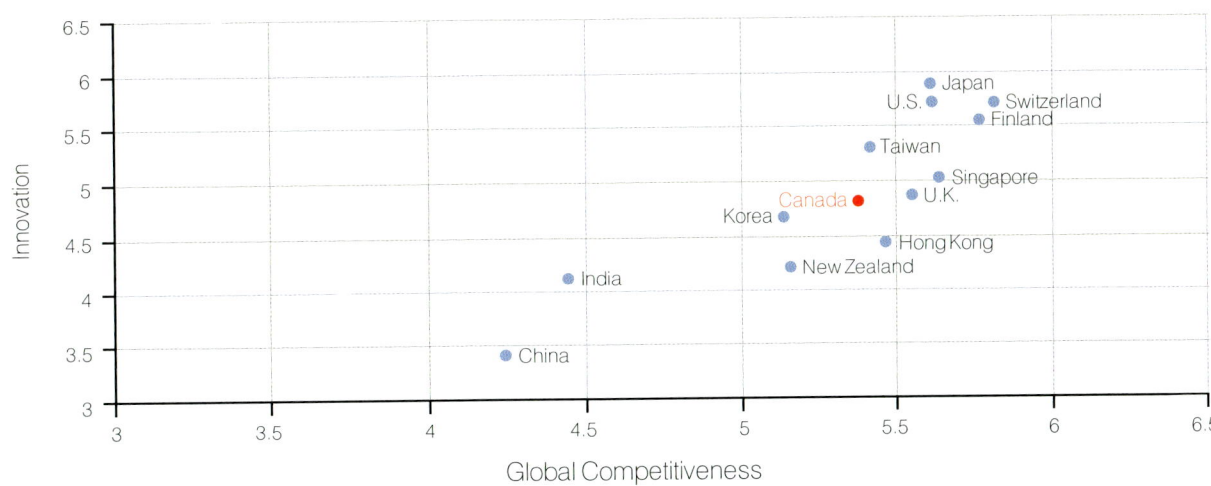

11 Graph of Competitiveness vs Innovation for Selected Countries (From World Economic Forum, Global Competitiveness Index, 2006)

This figure shows the relationship between national scores in global competitiveness and innovation. Innovation can be thought of as a measure of the design capability of a nation.

Country	Global Competitiveness Rank	Global Competitiveness Score	Innovation Rank	Innovation Score	Program	Status	Cost ($CDN)	Design Council	Design Centre(s)	Research	Competitions	Education	Branding / Marketing	Notes
Canada	16	5.37	13	4.82	None									
Singapore	5	5.63	9	5.04	Design Singapore	In progress		•	•			•	•	
South Korea	24	5.13	15	4.71	National Design Policy	In progress		•	•	•		•	•	3rd Five Year Plan will be completed in 2007
Other Asia Pacific Countries														
China	54	4.24	46	3.44										
Hong Kong	11	5.46	22	4.46										
India	43	4.44			National Design Policy	In final stages of approval		•	•			•	•	
Japan	7	5.6	1	5.9	Japan Design Foundation	Since 1983					•			
New Zealand	13	5.41	8	5.31	New Zealand Design Stategy	In progress since 2003	$10.1 million					•	•	A design council is being considered
Taiwan	13	5.41	8	5.31										
Other Countries														
Finland	2	5.76	4	5.56	Design 2005!	In progress	$40.9 million		•				•	2001-2006
Switzerland	1	5.81	3	5.72										
United Kingdom	10	5.54	12	4.89										
United States	6	5.61	2	5.72										

12 Table 1: Comparative Design Statistics and Activities

Towards a Design Nation

Outside the Asia Pacific Region, other countries have also embraced the idea of a design strategy—sometimes to great economic advantage. Finland, in particular, designated 2005 the Year of Design in Finland and invested $40.9 million CAD in design research, education, and promotion. As noted above, this investment in design has dramatically improved its global competitiveness.

Often these policies are managed, implemented, and promoted by government-created and supported organizations usually in the form of design councils. The United Kingdom formed its Design Council[13] in 1944 and it has made a significant contribution to that country (and to design in general) through the development of tools such as the Design Index mentioned above.

Korea also has a long history of government-supported design promotion. It established a Korean Design Packaging Centre in 1970, which became the Korean Institute of Design Promotion[14] in 2001. Singapore established its Design Singapore Council in 2003 under the auspices of the Ministry of Information, Communications and the Arts[15] and this organization leads the DesignSingapore Initiative, which hopes to position that country as a leading international centre for design and creativity.

Similarly, Japan has the Japan Industrial Design Promotion Organization (JIDPO)[16] which was established in 1969 by the Ministry of International Trade and Industry. Malaysia has the Malaysia Design Council[17] established in 1993. New Zealand has formed a Design in Business Strategy Group to explore the viability of a Design Council, and India plans to develop an India Design Council as part of its strategy.

These councils often set ambitious and significant economic targets. Korea anticipated that by 2007 its five-year plan would increase the value of design from 1.2 percent of the GDP in 2002 (or 7 trillion KRW, roughly $8.8 billion CAD) to 3 percent of the GDP and 20 trillion KRW ($25 billion CAD). New Zealand has set an objective called '5 x 50 x 500 x 5.' In the first five years of their plan they hope that at least fifty existing businesses will become internationally competitive through design and will generate an additional $500 million NZD ($406 million CAD) per year in export earnings. Moreover their objective is that this growth will continue at five times the targeted Gross Domestic Product growth rate to produce $1.5 billion NZD ($1.2 billion CAD) by the tenth year of the program. Similarly Singapore plans to use its Creative Industries Development Strategy to double that cluster's share of the GDP from 3 percent in 2000 to 6 percent in 2012. It is worth noting that in all cases this growth is predicated on growth in exports to countries such as Canada.

After World War II, Canada created a National Industrial Design Research Council to help manufacturers add value to export goods. In 1961 its mandate was broadened to include other design disciplines and was renamed the National Design Council. As a government body this group was responsible for policy issues and also represented Canada in organizations such as International Council of Societies of Industrial Design (ICSID).[18] At the same time, Industry Canada funded the creation of Design Canada in order to oversee the implementation of those policies. At the time of Expo 67 there was a great deal of interest

---

[13] www.designcouncil.org.uk

[14] www.designdb.com/english/kidp/index.asp

[15] www.designsingapore.com

[16] www.jidpo.or.jp/en/

[17] www.malaysiadesigncouncil.gov.my/

[18] www.icsid.org

in design in Canada but this gradually waned until both organizations were abolished in 1988 due to a general indifference to design.[19]

Design Centres are a physical manifestation of a country's design policies, a home for their design councils, and a point of presence to engage businesses, design professionals, and the general public. Again, many of the governments have already embraced this idea and have invested heavily in building such centres.[20]

In Seongnam City, just south of Seoul, the Republic of Korea has built an eight-storey design centre dubbed the New Millennium Design Ark. Distributed over 47,000 m², the centre includes an exhibit hall, a design experience museum, an e-design academy, an information centre, and an innovation centre with state-of-the-art equipment.

In its third five-year plan for design (2003-2007) Korea constructed regional design centres in Gwangju, Busan, and Daegu. The Gwangju Design Centre, for example, which opened in 2006, serves the southwestern part of the country and was built in partnership between the federal and municipal governments. It has an area of 17,000 m² distributed over eight floors. Built at a cost of 50 billion won or $62.7 million CAD, it includes an exhibition hall, a 300-seat event hall, and a variety of rapid prototyping tools.

Taiwan has invested $46 million NT ($1.6 million CAD) in its Taiwan Design Center of which the government provided two-thirds of the funding and the private sector the remaining one-third. It opened in 2004 and is located in Taipei. It includes a library, exhibition gallery, conference rooms, and rentable design studios.

Singapore has not developed a building specifically designated a Design Centre but it has invested heavily in the massive, thirty hectare Fusionopolis development. Fusionopolis is a live-work research and development complex for information, communications, and media industries. The overall intent is to use state-of-the-art facilities and technology to foster innovation, experimentation, and collaboration between public sector research institutes and private sector companies. Its first phase opened in 2008 and its key tenants are a variety of research institutes funded by the Agency for Science, Technology and Research (A*STAR), and the Media Development Authority (MDA). Phase one of the project opened in 2008 with 120,000 m² of space.

In addition to policies and infrastructure, design education is seen as an important means of promoting national design strategies. For example, five years ago China graduated only 1,500 industrial designers annually. Today it produces 10,000 at some 400 schools offering design courses. These new institutions represent a 2,000 percent increase in design schools since 1980. In recent years Tsinghua University in Beijing has opened a 60,000 m² design facility, and the Guangzhou Academy of Fine Arts has added an eight storey building which will expand its number of industrial design students fivefold to 3,000.[21] It should be pointed out, however, that many of these graduates are finding it difficult to find work and that many of the best students seek a period of study abroad.

19 This background information has been provided by John Arnott of the Arnott Design Group

20 In 1994, the Design Exchange (DX) was established in Toronto with $9 million of funding to develop a facility to promote Canadian design. Effectively the nation's design centre, the DX creates and hosts over fifty programs each year that illustrate the value of design and its critical link to the economy, environment, and quality of life. Despite serving as a model for other foreign design centres, however, it does not receive any operational support from the government to create and sustain its programs.

21 Business Week Online, www.businessweek.com/magazine/content/05_47/b3960003.htm, 11/21/05

In Singapore, four polytechnics and specialized art schools provide diploma level education in design. In 2001 some 2,300 students were registered in these design programs. The National University of Singapore offers degree programs in architecture and industrial design. The industrial design program is relatively new and produced its first group of about twenty graduates in 2003. One key strength of design education in Singapore is that its secondary schools include a mandatory course in design and technology. In 2005 the government also announced that it would open ten new specialty institutes in areas such as design and digital media.

During Korea's second Five Year Design Plan (1998-2002), the country was able to increase its number of graduates in design by 27 percent from 28,583 to 36,397. In its third Comprehensive Plan for Industrial Design Promotion (2003-2007), Korea is focusing on improving and enhancing its design education programs. This includes developing design education programs for teenagers; identifying and promoting young 'star' designers and facilitating their studies abroad; developing a design university certification process; and establishing education institutes for each design industry. In addition, Korea is increasingly embedding design education in a range of other disciplines, including business (design marketing), computing (multi-media design), and engineering programs, and is fostering stronger linkages between industry and design programs through funding for joint projects.

Beginning in 2003 as part of its four-year design strategy, the government of New Zealand announced that it would invest $1.2 million NZD ($973,000 CAD) in design education initiatives. This includes the development of design management courses and modules and managed industry internships for recent graduates.

The proposed National Design Policy for India would see various government agencies working in concert with private industry to graduate between 5,000 and 8,000 designers of all kinds annually with an annual growth rate of from 10 to 20 percent. In particular, it plans to expand and enhance the National Institute of Design (NID) in Ahmedabad and position it as a 'Global Centre of Excellence' in Design Education with a complete suite of design programs from the undergraduate to doctoral levels.

Because of the quality of its design education programs and because of the desire to study abroad by many of the best design students in the Asia Pacific region, Canada is well-positioned to export (and capitalize on) its expertise in this area through partnerships with existing institutions both here and abroad. At the same time, Canadian design professionals should note that in the future they will face increased competition from the thousands of designers that are now being educated elsewhere in the world.

Engaging the private sector remains a challenge, however, for all design strategies. In Canada and abroad most design firms are SMEs. At the same time, most SMEs lack the resources or understanding of how to use design as a competitive advantage. For this reason almost all of the national design strategies include a plan to facilitate the use of design by SMEs.

Singapore has a number of initiatives to help businesses develop their capabilities but the most relevant to design is operated by IE Singapore (International Enterprise Singapore) which offers grants of up to 50 percent of the costs of hiring a design consultant.

In Korea during the second Five-Year Plan, the government instituted a Design Consulting initiative that conducted 4,676 projects with SMEs. This was in addition to its Industrial Technology Development Fund that provided long-term low interest loans for SMEs to develop prototypes. Recently Korea began offering a one-stop service program to help commercialize and market promising designs.

Although not exclusively targeted at SMEs, New Zealand's Design Strategy includes some $7.95 million NZD ($6.4 million CAD) for Design Enable Initiatives that include a design audit and mentoring program and another called Design Project Number 1 which assists businesses carrying out their first design project.

As part of its national strategy, India hopes to target small-scale and cottage industries to sustain and strengthen the traditional knowledge, skills, and capabilities of its artisan-based workforce and to help modernize traditional crafts. To do this, it will encourage design education and training tailored to the needs of these SMEs through institutions such as the Indian Institutes of Technology and Management and its universities.

Without government assistance, China is leading the way in the effective engagement of SMEs through the emerging techniques of co-design and peer production mentioned above. Motorcycles in China are built by hundreds of SMEs that work together on design (co-design) and manufacturing (peer production) through local clusters supported by collaborative processes and standardized interfaces between modular components. The design process is rapid and iterative with suppliers taking joint responsibility for component compatibility. Motorcycle-makers specify only essential features, such as size and weight, and let outside designers improvise.[22] The effectiveness of this approach is demonstrated by the fact that while China exported only 500,000 motorcycles in 2000, it now produces half of the world's motorcycles.[23]

All of the countries referenced in this report understand the importance of branding as an economic enabler and recognize that this takes place at both a national and corporate level. The perception of 'German engineering,' for example, lends credibility to BMW even though close to 70 percent of each vehicle bearing their brand was designed and manufactured by a global network of suppliers such as Magna International.[24] And vice versa: for example, the reputation of Korea as a leading design location has grown in tandem with Samsung's reputation for well designed products. For this reason, Korea supports design research and development in its leading global firms, not just SMEs.

Similarly Singapore seeks to develop a 'New Asia' brand as an 'unique and exportable style' that would position Singapore as 'a gateway to the various cultures of Asia and a contemporary cosmopolitan city.'[25] At the same time, Korea's current five-year plan intends to 'enhance the image of Korea as a national brand.'[26] And India's nascent National Design Policy aims to '... position 'Designed

22 'Revving Up: Special Report on Innovation', **The Economist** (October 11, 2007)

23 D. Tapscott and A. D. Williams, **Wikinomics** (New York: Portfolio, 2007), 213-238; 'Revving Up: Special Report on Innovation', **The Economist** (October 11, 2007)

24 D. Tapscott and A. D. Williams, **Wikinomics** (New York: Portfolio, 2007), 231

25 'Design Singapore Initiative,' **The Creative Economy**. (Singapore: Ministry of Information, Communications and the Arts, 2003), 25. Available online at: www.mica.gov.sg/mica_business/attachment/ERC_SVS_CRE_Chapter3.pdf?sid=131&cid=1300.

26 KIDP Design Strategy Team. 'The 3rd Five-Year Plan' (Seoul: KIDP, 2005), 5. Available online at www.designdb.com/english/kidp/policy/policy.asp.

[27] Ministry of Commerce and Industry, India. 'Draft National Design Policy' (New Delhi: Ministry of Commerce and Industry, 2005), 2. Available online at www.designinindia.net/design-now/design-policy/index.html.

[28] A 2005 study of the impact of Korea's program found that product sales increased by an average of 22 times, and in one case, 200 times, after being bestowed the GD mark. The study was conducted by the Seoul National University Management Research Institute (personal communication, President of KAIST (Seoul), May 2007).

[29] www.10touchpoints.com.sg/phase1.aspx

[30] Chung, 11

in India' a by word [sic] for quality and utility.'[27] In each case these nations are prepared to invest in national and international branding and marketing strategies in order to achieve these goals.

In a number of cases this is to be accomplished through design awards and through the designation of certain products as embodying high quality design. Both Korea and Japan have adopted the 'good design mark' concept to recognize and promote well designed products, and India plans to establish an 'India Design Mark' soon.[28] Singapore initiated the President Design Awards, which focus on awarding excellence instead of minimum design standards. Singapore's strategy includes the identification and development of iconic Singapore products and services in areas such as hospitality and entertainment. And some nations have designated a Year of Design, such as Finland in 2005.

Another popular strategy uses design events to showcase local design capabilities, and expose designers to international competition and design trends. This usually includes organizing local design festivals and hosting international design exhibitions; showcasing local talent overseas through road shows; and supporting talented local designers' participation in internationally renowned design events.

Developing demand for good design is as essential to a design strategy as building design capacity, thus many countries are focusing on raising local awareness of the value of design. Design festivals and promotion of Good Design Marks are one way to increase the public's awareness of design. In addition, Korea has focused on raising design awareness among top management, with education programs such as the 'Design Executive Program' for CEOs, and works with the press to develop TV programs and in-depth reports on design to raise design consciousness more generally. Singapore has developed several innovative programs to increase the public's appreciation for design by soliciting their involvement, including '10 touch points', where the public is asked to submit entries and vote on what is worthy of redesign in the world around them.[29]

As a major market in its own right, the governments of both Korea and Singapore are leading by example by introducing a design focus to their own government procurement practices and projects. Singapore's Urban Redevelopment Authority (URA) is a leader in this respect, emphasizing good design in physical planning, from conceptual to street level.

Clearly governments do have a role to play in these initiatives. Kyung Won Chung has pointed out that, 'For developing countries such as Korea, a close rapport between government and the civilian sector can be the most important factor for the success of design promotion.'[30] In fact, in both developed and developing nations, public sector support is necessary because of the unique nature of the design industries. Design is practiced largely by SMEs who typically have neither the resources nor expertise to engage in research or promotion. Government assistance is also required to 'jumpstart' a culture of research to address critical design issues such as sustainability. It should also be recognized that issues such as sustainability are a public good, not a source of profit, and require the kind of long-term investment that does not necessarily attract venture capital.

For these reasons Chung has suggested a government-pull and civilian-push model which is worth quoting in detail:

> The design promotion process begins with some form of government initiative followed by a variety of civilian design activities. The establishment of a national design promotion organization, can start the process. The design society provides the promotional organization with professional support and advice for establishing appropriate design infrastructures as well as strategies. Then the two parties collaborate closely in preparing a comprehensive scenario for successful design promotion, after which the process goes into a continuous spin of close interaction between the government-funded design promotion organization and the professional design associations ...[31]

[31] Ibid, 10

RECOMMENDATIONS

Design provides the means to make Canada more productive, competitive, and sustainable. It means more energy-efficient, environmentally friendly, and effective goods and services and as such, design can increase the export of Canadian products. Other countries, however, provide a striking contrast to Canada in the extent of their commitment to design quality and their support for design as an instrument of public policy.

What is clear is that strategic economic and social advantages accrue to countries that embrace and endorse high quality design. Investments by governments in design have been consistently validated by measurable increases in their capacity for innovation and their competitiveness in global markets. To remain competitive in the twenty-first century, Canada must brand itself as a 'Design Nation.' This is a long term process but it begins with the discussion and development of a pan-Canadian design strategy.

While it is beyond the scope of this document to describe such a strategy in detail, the material provided here does provide a means to learn from the experiences of other countries. In particular, Canada's design strategy should be elaborated on multiple fronts. As countries such as Singapore and South Korea demonstrate, Canada should create a demand for high-quality design while simultaneously building the capacity to meet that demand. Those experiences also suggest that a design strategy should be developed as an active partnership of the academic, private, and public sectors.

Engaging the relevant stakeholders is a critical first step in this process. All levels of government and multiple departments should participate. Design, manufacturing, and development firms of all sizes should be involved, as should software developers and hardware vendors. Researchers, educators, design professionals, contractors, manufacturers, and trades people will also have valuable insights into the crafting of such a strategy. As a key receptor community, business people (and those involved in SMEs in particular) should play an active role. Finally, the general public should be consulted since it appears that the best means to raise the quality of design in Canada is to create an ongoing demand for it.

Active engagement of appropriate communities is important for a variety of reasons. Canada does have a unique cultural, historical, and geographic context that is different from other countries. What constitutes an effective design strategy in those countries may not be successful in this country. Proposed strategies must be developed and tested through consultation with relevant user groups.

As mentioned, the general public plays an essential role in the development of Canada as a 'Design Nation.' Again and again in the course of this study it was noted that an awareness and appreciation of good design by non-designers—consumers—is critical to the creation of new opportunities for designers. Raise the level of expectation, we were told repeatedly, and Canadian designers will rise to the challenge. This must start by developing demand for good design at home, in both the private and public sectors.

A demand for high-quality design can be created through a vigorous program of design promotion. As noted, Korea used a 'push-pull' model to create an ongoing feedback loop of design activities that is put in motion by the government but which responds to and is directed by designers, business people, and the general public. Moreover, these promotional strategies need to be of a significant and prolonged nature to effectively change perceptions.

There are a number of ways this can occur. In terms of demand, all government levels must lead by example by making good design part of their procurement process and projects; government assistance is needed to promote design to the general public through exhibits, design competitions, and award programs that celebrate excellence; research is needed to measure the value of design (such as the creation of a Canadian Design Index based on the U.K. model); and SMEs need government support, through funding and joint research, to raise awareness of the value of design, and to develop their own design capabilities. Singapore's integrated approach, in which all design disciplines are coordinated by a single government ministry (the Ministry of Information Communications and the Arts), should also be carefully studied.

At the same time, given the country's need for an enhanced design reputation, the strategy should also focus on building up an international profile through participation in international design events and the creation of networks, associations, and collaborations that can give firms—and particularly SMEs—a greater international presence.

Concomitant with this program of design promotion, Canada must also expand and enhance its design capacity. Again it is emphasized that it is beyond the scope of this report to create a detailed plan for each of these areas but Canada needs to respond to current trends in education, practice, and infrastructure. For example, many design schools are moving towards graduate degrees but need support from government and industry to effectively transition to research-based environments. At the same time professional design organizations are placing a greater emphasis on continuing education. In both cases e-learning offers a method of meeting these growing needs. Technology presents its own challenges. Designers, design researchers, and design students all must access the latest technology but are hindered by the high capital and operating costs associated with new equipment—particularly if they are an SME. New approaches to the sharing of, and access to tools, are needed and again these may be facilitated by high speed telecommunications.

By learning from the examples of other countries and by strategic funding of both design promotion and capacity, Canada could quickly and significantly improve its current global status particularly in terms of innovation. In this new century, Canada must recognize and realize the value of design to become more productive, sustainable, and competitive.

Afterword

Why Ourtopias? Why hold a conference on the future of design? What do we learn from three days of presentations and discussion? Answers to such questions may be self-evident to designers. Perhaps though, the broader world might struggle to understand just how important are events like Ourtopias. There can be no doubt that the decisions designers, planners and the political process take have profound impact on the quality of our lives. The complexity, scope and scale of urban design and building means that many of its effects cannot be treated in isolation, cannot be prototyped in advance. Designers do not have the luxury of controlled experimentation, of extended prototypes or beta-releases. We must work in the moment and our work is both used immediately and persists for many years. In design, we learn largely in retrospect and through extended discussion that connects past ideas, through current work to future directions. In June 2007, Ourtopias provided a wonderful ground for such debate. Its highlights included an astounding presentation on the remaking of Toronto's cultural venues (Bruce Kuwabara), a probing retrospective of the continuing impact of Expo 67 on Canadian design thinking (Dr. Annmarie Adams of McGill University), a deep analysis of the role of goal-oriented non-profit organization in social housing (David Hughes, Habitat for Humanity) and sharp insight into the political process that is a necessary part of realizing great design (Glen Murray). These four presentations are only symbols for the diversity and robustness of the debates during Ourtopias. I have little doubt that attendees left transformed, with new insights into design and its effectiveness in the world. The Design Exchange plays a key role in the absolutely necessary process of public debate and learning about design. We are all richer for its continuing advocacy for and examination of Canadian design.

Robert Woodbury, BArch, MSc, PhD
Scientific Director, Canadian Design Research Network
Professor, Simon Fraser University

Publication Credits

PUBLICATION DIRECTOR   Philip Beesley
ART DIRECTOR   Hayley Isaacs
COPY EDITING   Daniela Bryson, AnneMarie Minardi, Catherine Molnar, Katie Weber

KUWABARA   Ourtopia: Ideal Cities and the Role of Design in Remaking Urban Space

- 1,5,7,10   Tom Arban, photographer
- 2   Image by Gother Mann
- 4   Diagram by Kuwabara Payne McKenna Blumberg Architects
- 6   Peter Sellar, photographer
- 8,12,14-15   Rendering by Kuwabara Payne McKenna Blumberg Architects
- 11   Photographer, Thomas Struth, Courtesy of the artist and Marian Goodman Gallery, New York
- 13   Shai Gil, photographer

WHITE   Condomania! Condominium Culture and Cities of Convenience

- 2   Toronto Life Cover Photograph: Derek Shapton
- 6   Image by OMA

MCARTHUR   John M. Lyle and the Civic Improvement Committee

- 1,2,6,10,11,17,19-23,27,28   Images courtesy of Glenn McArthur
- 16   Glenn McArthur, photographer

CHODIKOFF	Fringe Benefits: Cosmopolitan Dynamics of a Multicultural City
1,2,4,7,12-15	Ian Chodikoff, photographer

SEEBOHM, DANAHY	Towards Constructive Dialogue: Real-Time Visualization and Geographic Information Systems
1	John Danahy, photographer
2,4-5,13,15	Rendering by John Danahy
3,14,18	Rendering by Thomas Seebohm
9	Peter Bosselman, photographer, Representation of Places. (Berkeley: University of California Press, 1998)
12,16	Rendering by Bill Chan
20	Rendering by Marjorie Clark

VERA, YESHAYAHU	From Urban Cell to Global Hive
2,4-5	Images by Maria del C. Vera and Shai Yeshayahu

KOLODZIEJ	Genius Loci: The Need for Urban Scenography
1-15	Drawings and photographs by Adam Kolodziej

KIRKPATRICK	Landscape Manufacturing
2	Image by OMA/Bruce Mau

HARDWICKE	Ravine City and Farm City
2,4,6-7,9-10	Images and renderings by Chris Hardwicke

Biographies

Philip Beesley

Philip Beesley practices art and architecture in Waterloo and Toronto, Canada. He is an Associate Professor at the University of Waterloo, School of Architecture in Cambridge, Ontario. He is responsible for the dissemination and publication programs of the Canadian Design Research Network. He co-directs Waterloo's Integrated Centre for Manufacturing, Visualization and Design, a facility combining high-performance computing and automated manufacturing of architectural components. He was educated in architecture at the University of Toronto, in visual art at Queen's University and in technology at Humber College. Distinctions for his work include the Prix de Rome in Architecture (Canada). Publications include Fabrication: Examining the Digital Practice of Architecture (AIA/ACADIA 2004), Responsive Architectures: Subtle Technologies (Riverside, 2006), Future Wood (Riverside, 2006), Mobile Nation (Riverside, 2007), and On Growth And Form: Organic Architecture and Beyond (TUNS Press 2007).

Ian Chodikoff

Ian Chodikoff is an architect and the editor of Canadian Architect magazine. With a background in political science, he holds graduate degrees in architecture and urban design from the University of British Columbia and Harvard University respectively. He has undertaken projects ranging from the relationship between the natural and man-made influences of urban parks to the effects of social inclusion and community diversity on urban design. Since May 2006, he has helped facilitate a series of charrettes and presentations with the City of Toronto and the Design Exchange to improve the built environment in several priority neighbourhoods across Toronto. He is currently working on a project entitled 'Fringe Benefits: Cosmopolitan Dynamics of a Multicultural City' where he will be curating an ongoing exhibition exploring the effects of multiculturalism on Toronto's suburban communities. He has lectured in various universities and cities across North America and Europe, has served on numerous juries and has written in a variety of magazines and journals on issues ranging from planning and sustainability. Committed to the profession, he has served on committees including the Toronto Society of Architects, the Royal Architectural Institute of Canada, as well as having been a consultant with the Canada Council for the Arts on the subject of architectural competitions.

David Covo

David Covo is an architect and Associate Professor of Architecture at McGill University. His teaching, research and professional interests include barrier-free design, residential design, low-cost housing, representation and architectural sketching, and have led to assignments in Pakistan, China, Mexico, Romania, Singapore and Korea. A Member of the Order of Architects of Quebec and a Fellow of the Royal Architectural Institute of Canada, he served as Director of the School of Architecture from 1996 to 2007, as president of the Canadian Architectural Certification Board from 2002 to 2004, and is a member of the Board of the Canadian Design Research Network (CDRN).

John Danahy

John Danahy has developed an internationally recognized expertise in digital media for design, planning and visualization. He teaches landscape architecture, urban design, planning, architecture, and computer science. He has lead the development of research software systems at the Centre for Landscape Research (CLR) and been a pioneer in the use of computing and virtual reality in urban design and landscape architectural practice. He is Director of the CLR, an executive committee member of the Knowledge Media Design Institute (KMDI) and a founding member of the CDRN.

Chris Hardwicke

Chris Hardwicke has always pursued the clarity of big ideas. As an associate at Sweeny Sterling Finlayson & Co Architects, Chris is in charge of city building projects such as the Toronto Waterfront Projects, the Toronto Gateway Project, and the Waterfront Master Plan for Kaohsiung, Taiwan. His visionary ideas and projects have been presented at the Milan Furniture Fair, Grand Central Station, the University of Art and Design in Helsinki, Doors of Perception 07 in India and published in the books The Good Life: New Spaces for Recreation and uTOpia: Towards a New Toronto.

James Kirkpatrick

James Kirkpatrick holds a Bachelor of Landscape Architecture from Guelph University, and a Masters of Architecture from the University of British Columbia. His thesis project, 'Celeb', inspired simultaneously by Guy Debord and Britney Spears, was an analysis of the devices of celebrity as image within the architectural design process. He is currently researching the critical potential of landscape as image through recent design projects for orphan spaces in Toronto and the Hobart Waterfront, and an upcoming exhibition on landscape as generator of urban form. He has been involved in academics at Guelph, Waterloo, and Ryerson Universities. He is Associate Director of Urban Design at EDAW in London.

Adam Kolodziej

Adam Kolodziej arrived in Canada in 1984 from Krakow, Poland. With his background in architecture (M.Arch from Krakow University of Technology) and the arts (M.A., Academy of Fine Arts), he has been working as an Art Director, Production Designer for film and television, and Theatre Designer. In 1987 he won the Pauline McGibbon Award for outstanding theatre design and has also been nominated for a Dora Award and a Gemini Award. Since 2004, he has been Assistant Professor with the School of Interior Design, Faculty of Communication and Design, Ryerson University, Toronto. Elected member of the Royal Canadian Academy of Arts, member of Directors Guild of Canada, the Canadian Academy of Cinema and Television and member of ARIDO (Association of Registered Interior Designers of Ontario).

Bruce Kuwabara

Bruce Kuwabara is a founding partner of Kuwabara Payne McKenna Blumberg Architects and the 2006 recipient of the RAIC Gold Medal for Architecture. He studied architecture at the University of Toronto. Upon graduation he joined the studio of George Baird, an architect and theorist who was influential to Kuwabara's interest in urban revitalization and the history of the city. In 1975 he joined Barton Myers Associates where he worked for over 12 years and as an associate led high profile design competitions for Phoenix City Hall in Arizona. During this time he explored ideas of creating civic landscapes and building the public realm that he would later further evolve in projects with KPMB, including the winning scheme for Kitchener City Hall. These core principles continue to inform his work, and are most recently evidenced in his work on several of Toronto's cultural renaissance projects, including the Celia Franca Centre for Canada's National Ballet School (a joint venture with Goldsmith Borgal & Company), the Gardiner Museum renewal, and the new home for the Toronto International Film Festival Group.

Richard Levy

Dr. Richard Levy is a Professor of Planning and Urban Design at the University of Calgary. Since 1996, Dr.. Levy has also served as Director of Computing for the Faculty of EVDS. He is a founding member of the Virtual Reality Lab. Dr.. Levy speaks at international and national conferences in the fields of virtual reality, 3D imaging, education, archaeology and planning. His published work appears in journals such as Internet Archaeology, IEEE MultiMedia, Journal of Visual Studies, Environment and Planning and Plan Canada.

Douglas MacLeod

Douglas MacLeod is currently the Executive Director of the Okanagan Science and Technology Council and the Executive Director of the Canadian Design Research Network. He is also a registered architect and a contributing editor to Canadian Architect. He has degrees in architecture and computer science from the University of Toronto and a Masters degree in Environmental Design from the University of Calgary.

Glenn McArthur

Glenn McArthur is a designer, photographer, author and artist, whose work has been exhibited in major Ontario galleries. He has worked as a graphic designer for top advertising agencies and design studios in both New York City and Toronto. His 1996 book on the architect William Thomas that was published by Carlton University Press and which, in addition to his writing, featured his photography, drawings and design, received glowing reviews and numerous awards including one from Heritage Toronto. His current book project, The Architecture of John M. Lyle, 1872-1945: A Progressive Traditionalist is pending publication with Coach House Press.

Larissa Muller

Dr. Larissa Muller is an Assistant Professor of Environmental Design and the Planning Program Coordinator at the University of Calgary. Her research and consulting work over the last fifteen years has focused on economic and spatial development strategies at national and regional scales, predominantly in Asian country contexts, as well as in the United States and Canada. She holds a PhD in Urban and Regional Planning from the University of California, Berkeley.

Catherine Molnar

Catherine Molnar is the Professional Programs Coordinator at Design Exchange. She previously worked in the City of Toronto's Museums Department and Culture Division, helping to coordinate Doors Open Toronto and co-curate online exhibits, including the award-winning 'History of Toronto: An 11,000-Year Journey'. Her other recent Toronto-related curated exhibits include 'Oak Street Reinvented' (Cabbagetown/Regent Park Museum; 2007) and 'Girls on the Homefront' (Havergal College/Virtual Museum of Canada; 2008). Catherine has a Master of Arts in English from the University of York's (UK) Centre for Eighteenth-Century Studies. She completed doctoral coursework in Canadian History at York University before joining Design Exchange in 2007.

Paola Poletto

Paola Poletto is Senior Director of Development and Special Projects at Design Exchange, Canada's national center for design. Prior to this new appointment in 2008, she was Senior Director of Programs, responsible for youth and professional programs, exhibitions and the museum collection. Paola brings over twelve years of experience in arts administration in national and international organizations, and an additional five years of content development and management for print and new media. Since 2001, she has provided strategic direction for digifest, an international festival of design and media culture produced by Design Exchange in partnership with the Ontario Science Centre and Harbourfront Centre. digifest 2005 included a programming initiative showcasing Canadian design at Expo 2005, Japan; and in 2003, a comprehensive e-learning website featuring designers and artists concerned with the future of cities. In 2008, she co-led and launched a research report on product design and development with

Industry Canada. Artist-led projects include Kiss Machine (kissmachine.org) from 2000-2005, Inflatable Museum (2001-4), Girls and Guns (Toronto-London, 2003; Budapest-Albania-Montenegro & Serbia, 2004), and Boredom Fighters! (Tightrope Books, 2008).

Samantha Sannella

Samantha Sannella is currently the President and CEO of the Design Exchange, Canada's Design Museum. She is responsible for leading the organization in their mandate to increase awareness of the critical link between business and design. Ms. Sannella is a former professor of Interior Design at Ryerson University and a former practice leader for HOK Consulting Canada. Her expertise includes strategic planning, architectural and interior design for Fortune 500 companies. As part of her career, Ms. Sannella has been instrumental to organizations through fundraising, public relations and community involvement. Ms. Sannella is passionate about Universal Design and Sustainable Design and teaches audiences about the critical connections between design, health and well-being, the economy and the environment. Ms. Sannella is also considered an expert in designing for and marketing to the Multi-Generational workplace and has traveled around the world as a conference speaker for this subject. In 2006, Ms. Sannella was named one of the top 10 most inspiring women in Canada. In 2007, she was honoured by Ryerson University for her work within the design community. She serves on the advisory committee for Sheridan School of Interior Design, Humber School of Industrial Design and is on the advisory board of IIDEX NeoCon Canada.

Thomas Seebohm

Thomas Seebohm's research interests involve digital technology to design a more holistically conceived architecture and urban environment. A special focus of his research is digital urban design and the use of 3D, real-time, virtual city models for designing livable cities with community participation. He has also been involved in the linking of Geographic Information Systems (GIS) data with computer aided design (CAD), and in particular the generation of 3D models from GIS mapping and attribute data. Thomas is a registered architect, a professional engineer and an associate professor of architecture at the University of Waterloo.

Akin Sevinc

Dr. Akin Sevinc is a writer, architect and researcher living in Istanbul. He studied architecture at the Istanbul Technical University, where he completed his PhD. He currently teaches architectural design and architectural utopias at the Yeditepe University Architecture Department. He is the author of books such as Utopya: Hayali Ahali Projesi (Utopia: No/w/here Projects, 2005) and Dunyanin Yan Etkileri (Side Effects of the World, 2006). His research interests include literature, imaginary spaces and utopias. He has lectured in various schools and cities across Europe and has written in a variety of magazines and journals. Dr. Sevinc is currently writing a novel and completing a research book on architectural dreams.

Maria del C. Vera

Maria del C. Vera received her Master of Architecture in Urban Culture from Universitat Politècnica de Catalunya. She has taught in design studios abroad and in the USA. Presently, she teaches at Southern Illinois University. Her research stems from the realization that life is fundamentally sustainable. As Principal and Co-Founder of VerS, two of her most notable endeavors are: House @ -1˚ latitude 81˚ featured in the Atlas of Contemporary World Architecture and Zero Budget (Ecuador). Beyond teaching and practice she is involved in a collaborative effort to identify human hegemony.

Mason White

Mason White received his Master of Architecture from Harvard's Graduate School of Design in 2001. He has worked in offices in New York and London, UK. Mason initiated Lateral Architecture in 2002 as an experimental design studio focusing on architecture and urbanism. He was the Lefevre Fellow at Ohio State University 2004-05, and received the Young Architects Award from the Architectural League of New York in 2005. Mason currently teaches at the University of Toronto Faculty of Architecture Landscape and Design.

Robert F. Woodbury

Professor Robert Woodbury holds a Bachelor of Architecture from Carleton University where he was awarded the Lieutenant Governor's Silver Medal in Architecture in 1981. He earned his Master of Science and PhD from Carnegie Mellon University. He was a faculty member in Architecture and the Engineering Design Research Center at Carnegie Mellon University from 1982 to 1993, at Adelaide University in South Australia from 1993 to 2001, at the Technical University of British Columbia from 2001 to 2002 and is now at Simon Fraser University. He was founding Chair of the Graduate Program in the School of Interactive Arts and Technology at SFU and a founding member of the Master of Digital Media program jointly offered by four Vancouver institutions. From 2005-2008 he was Scientific Director of the Canadian Design Research Network, the national association of design researchers in Canada.

Shai Yeshayahu

Shai Yeshayahu obtained a MArch from Ohio State University. He has lived in Brazil, Ecuador, Spain, Italy and Israel and in 2004 joined the School of Architecture at Southern Illinois University where he founded the Digital Fabrication Lab and implemented a digital culture across the curriculum. He is co-founder of VerS, a design research practice responsive to ancient, emerging, and local data. Shai is collaborating with artists, computer scientists and biologists on an interactive installation that deploys sensors to the built environment. His research focuses on methodologies that employ novel usage of technology to create a backdrop for creative thinking.